# No One Like Him

# Other books by Thomas A. Jones

*Mind Change: The Overcomer's Handbook*

*Letters to New Disciples*

*God's Perfect Plan for Imperfect People*

*To Live Is Christ*
(coauthored with Sheila Jones)

*The Prideful Soul's Guide to Humility*
(coauthored with Michael Fontenot)

# No One Like Him

## Jesus and His Message

### THOMAS A. JONES

**DPI**
DISCIPLESHIP
PUBLICATIONS
INTERNATIONAL

**No One Like Him**

© 2002 Discipleship Publications International

2 Sterling Rd., Billerica, Mass., 01862-2595

Printed in the United States of America

ISBN: 1-57782-180-7

*Cover and Interior Design: Jennifer Matienzo*

*In memory of Ryan Howard, my friend for more than twenty years and a man whose passion for Jesus was evident to all*

# Contents

**Introduction**
*Jesus: The Hinge of Your History* . . . . . . . . . . . . . . . . 8

1   Who Did He Think He Was? . . . . . . . . . . . . . . . . 12

2   His Dependence on God . . . . . . . . . . . . . . . . . . 25

3   His Servant Heart . . . . . . . . . . . . . . . . . . . . . 36

4   Rich in Character . . . . . . . . . . . . . . . . . . . . . 47

5   Jesus and the Scriptures . . . . . . . . . . . . . . . . . 58

6   The Kingdom of God . . . . . . . . . . . . . . . . . . . 68

7   His Good News: Extravagant Generosity . . . . . . . . 86

8   Kingdom Attitudes . . . . . . . . . . . . . . . . . . . . 95

9   The Kingdom Lifestyle . . . . . . . . . . . . . . . . . . 111

10  Conflict and Controversy . . . . . . . . . . . . . . . . 125

11  Even Death on a Cross . . . . . . . . . . . . . . . . . . 137

12  The Empty Tomb . . . . . . . . . . . . . . . . . . . . . 151

13  Disciples of Jesus . . . . . . . . . . . . . . . . . . . . . 161

14  But Does It Work? . . . . . . . . . . . . . . . . . . . . . 170

**Epilogue**
*What Will You Do?* . . . . . . . . . . . . . . . . . . . . . . 176

**Notes** . . . . . . . . . . . . . . . . . . . . . . . . . . . . . . 182

*Introduction*

# Jesus : The Hinge of Your History

In one of the most vivid memories of my early adulthood, I recall sitting at the dinner table one night with my parents and hearing my father ask me why I looked so unhappy. He reminded me of how well things had gone for our family in recent years and how much I had to be grateful for. "How can you feel like this," he asked, "with all you have?" Exactly what I said in reply is less clear to me, but I remember muttering something about not really understanding it all.

Some months later, I decided that my problem was a fairly "minor" one: I had not really found meaning for my life. Somehow accomplishments in school, my car and my frequent afternoons on the golf course were not satisfying a growing hunger. At nineteen, I had an easy life, but I was still trying to figure out how to live. As I look back, I feel blessed that I was troubled. Those feelings led me some months later to begin a journey that would result in what I will write about in this book.

I don't think my need was unique. At the heart of every human life there is one fundamental question that begs to be answered: "How can I really live?" My guess is that you, too, have asked or do ask this question, in one form or another. My goal with this book is to help you answer it.

This book is not just information about a most interesting man who started a movement a long time ago. And it is more than a book about an ancient man who disturbed his culture or did something to become famous. This book is about a man who is still teaching us how to live. It is about a man who can give us confidence while keeping us humble. It is about a man who can give us security even while there are thousands of things we have not yet figured out. In a world that offers us a multitude of choices and tells us we need to be a dozen different things, this book takes us to a man who shows us what really matters. It is about a man who teaches us how to connect with God and how to love others.

In Thomas Cahill's best-selling series *The Hinges of History*, he describes individuals or groups who gave a gift to the world that left it a far different place. The third book in his series of seven projected volumes is about Jesus of Nazareth.[1] I would go further than Cahill and suggest that Jesus is, in fact, *the* hinge of history, but more than that, I am going to suggest in this book that he can be the hinge of your personal history, meaning his life can represent a genuine turning point for you. There is a fundamental premise behind this book—namely, the more you know about Jesus, the more you will know about life. And this is why Jesus is *must* reading. I challenge you to test my premise.

If you have never studied the life of Jesus before, you will need to supplement what you read here with the primary sources for his life—the four unique Gospels of Matthew, Mark, Luke and John. Hopefully, what you find here will inspire you to dig deep into those documents. If this is the fifth or fiftieth book you have read about Jesus, I am confident that you can still benefit from what is here, if you read with an eager heart and open mind. As I have learned again in working on this book, even those of us who think we know the Jesus story well, still have much more to learn.

After twenty years of following Jesus, the Apostle Paul would still write: "I want to know Christ" (Philippians 3:10). The message of Jesus is simple enough to help a child, but deep enough to challenge the greatest of minds—and keep them coming back for more. But perhaps the most amazing thing about Jesus is this: even if this book about him tells you nothing that you do not already know, you will benefit from reading again things about him you have heard and have comprehended. He is so full of truth and life that no encounter with him is wasted. There are stories in the Gospels that I have read hundreds of times, and yet a fresh reading of one of these may make all the difference in how I handle my day.

Jesus is the absolute center of the Christian faith. Everything about it is dependent on who he is and what he did, and yet many who claim to be Christians are woefully ignorant about Jesus. For this reason, our first goal in this book is to destroy myths and misconceptions and bring us face to face with the real Jesus. If you are still trying to make some decision about him, you need the facts, and I want to challenge you to be relentless in your pursuit of them. Don't accept vague generalities. Get the specifics. Find out what Jesus actually did. Find out what he actually said. Get to know what the man was really like. Only then can you make an informed decision.

But there is another goal I have in writing this book: to present the Jesus who will train us to live. Jesus was a teacher. Training was in his blood. If you are willing to sit humbly at Jesus' feet as a student, I am convinced that you will learn how to live. You will leave this study with a deeper sense of who you should be.

Jesus' original disciples followed him and listened to him and watched him, and in the process were trained by him in how to live. They learned both how to have right hearts on the inside and how to do what is right on the outside. People don't just accidentally become successful at living life; they have to be trained. Ball players need training. Engineers and doctors need training. Teachers need training. Sadly, we train people to do everything but live. People need training. People who want to live fully need training in how to do it. This is what Jesus did. He trained men and women to live, and the goal of this book is to present the Jesus who trains us and equips us to be what we are supposed to be.

If your mind is open and your heart is willing, if you are ready to come to grips with life, then let's move on with the attitude of the inquisitive Greeks who came to Jesus' disciples saying, "Sir, we would like to see Jesus" (John 12:21).

# 1
# Who Did He Think He Was?

**W**hat can we infer about the man from Nazareth when almost 2,000 years after his birth, one of the most popular news magazines in the world puts this question on its cover: "Who Was Jesus?"[1] What does it say when the three leading news magazines in the United States have had a cover story featuring Jesus at least seven times in twelve years? When an itinerant teacher from a tiny Palestinian hamlet still draws the attention of our modern, thoroughly secularized society, we have to say that it is remarkable. These culturally sensitive publications, which always have an eye on the bottom line, are not known for featuring irrelevant cover stories. We know we are dealing with someone incredibly unique when we consider how durable the man and his message have been through the years. Jesus simply will not go away.

But the question raised on the cover of *Time* is a good one, no, a vital one. Who was Jesus? Or even better, who is Jesus? How do we identify him? Was he a good man who was misunderstood? Was he an outwardly religious fellow with hidden political agendas? Was he one of those clever deceivers who comes along every so often and draws the affections and contributions of the weak and the naive? Or was he something different, something more? Was there something about him that made him unlike anyone else? Is there evidence that he is without comparison or analogy? Was God in this man like he had never been in any man before? If you are ready, let us together go after the facts.

The whole idea of the Christian faith is built on the concept that Jesus has a positively unique identity—that he was, in fact, totally unlike any prophet, priest or preacher who had ever lived or would ever live afterward. Let us make an absurd comparison in order to make a point here. In one sense, Adolf Hitler occupies a unique place in world history. There have been other tyrants and diabolical figures, and there will be more if the world endures, but in the minds of most people, he stands as the worst. His name is synonymous with ruthlessness, atrocity and the most heinous use of state power. Certainly there are others, like Joseph Stalin, who are not far behind him in our thinking—and in reality, they may have been just as bad or worse. So in most of our minds, Hitler is unique, but not totally unique. He stands alone, but somewhat arguably. As bad a man as he was, there are others who may have come close to reaching his level of evil and may have even equaled it.

But now turn the coin of evil and good over and consider Jesus. There have been others who have pointed men to God. There have been others who have had compassion for the poor and the disenfranchised. There have been others who have courageously refused to compromise and have spoken out boldly against abuses, even when it brought persecution or death. But the assertion of the New Testament is that there is still no one in Jesus' league—no one who even comes close. The claim itself is quite remarkable, actually being made about no other significant religious leader in the history of the world. And so we must ask if there is any basis for what might be considered by some to be a completely outrageous claim.

## A Real Man

In the cold war days, when the Soviet Union was so entrenched in an ideological defense of atheism, the massive *Great Soviet Encyclopedia*, with its fifty-six volumes, contained only a two-line reference to Jesus of Nazareth: "Jesus: the mythological founder of Christianity."[2] Jesus was given a place right alongside Hermes, Zeus, Prometheus and Paul Bunyan. He was seen as a man whose name appeared in ancient stories, but who was only a legend. Such a statement was, as Bruce Metzger, a New Testament scholar, points out, a reflection of the old Soviet propaganda, and no serious historian today would identify Jesus as a mythological figure. Whatever scholars disagree on, they are united in the fact that Jesus lived, taught his message in Palestine and died in that environment.[3]

Tacitus, an official first century historian of the Roman Empire, who had access to all the records of capital punishment, tells us that "Christus" was put to death under the procurator Pontius Pilate in the province of Judea. Josephus, the Jewish historian, who also wrote under the auspices of the Roman government, refers in his writings to John the Baptist and to Jesus, and to the fact that Jesus was the "so-called Christ."[4]

In addition to these non-Christian sources, there is the whole first century Christian movement that shook the Roman Empire with its abundance of testimony by disciples who were eyewitnesses to Jesus' life and teaching. Without the historical reality of Jesus, there would never have been a movement at all.

So Jesus really existed. About this there is no doubt. But who was he or who is he? How should we label him? What titles should we give him? Perhaps the best place to start is with his own view of himself, which undoubtedly tells us much about a man. Once we know more about how he viewed himself, we will be in a better position to make our own judgment about him. For example, if you were to come to my home for a meal, spend time with my family and me and watch a favorite movie of mine, you might conclude that I am a nice middle class fellow who could be relied on if there was a need. But suppose I told you privately, as I walked you to the door, that I had complete knowledge about all the comings and goings of the 40,000 people in my suburban Boston town? To hear me tell it, there was not one thing that happened to any of them that I did not know. Certainly, this would cause some major rethinking of your first impression of me. The options you would consider in regard to me would now be strikingly different. With Jesus we will run into something very much like this.

## Troubling Ideas

Some of Jesus' statements indicate that he saw himself as having a unique purpose, but they were all statements we could fit into Biblical tradition. Early in Mark's Gospel we learn that Jesus had a strong sense of mission. He saw himself as a man with a message that needed to be preached. "Jesus replied, 'Let us go somewhere else—to the nearby villages—so I can preach there also. That is why I have come'" (Mark 1:38). He believed that he understood truth that others needed to grasp and that it was his responsibility to proclaim it. Of course, he was not the first to feel the same calling.

It seems that he took another step when he began to use the term "prophet." In Mark we have the well-known reference to a prophet being without honor among his own people (Mark 6:1–5). Jesus is obviously referring to himself here. He was well aware of the way the Jews used the word "prophet." He did not use it lightly in reference to himself. He saw himself as a messenger from God, as is further evidenced in Luke 13:31–33 when he again refers to himself by saying, "Surely no prophet can die outside of Jerusalem!" This idea is confirmed in John 14:24 when Jesus says, "These words you hear are not my own; they belong to the Father who sent me."

However, there was a difference in the way Old Testament prophets spoke and the way Jesus spoke. They would say, "This is what the Lord says" (more majestically put in the older versions as, "Thus saith the Lord"). Jesus, on the other hand, would say, "I tell you the truth." This appears in the Greek New Testament as *"Amen, Amen,"* which means "truly, truly." While this may sound perfectly acceptable to our ears, it was shocking to Jesus' hearers. To the Jewish people the message was clear: he was claiming to be able to speak on his own—something that was without parallel among the rabbis of Jesus' time.

We also see an unprecedented focus on himself in his message, as in the quiet and reassuring invitation that Jesus gave to the crowds: "Come to *me*, all you who are weary and burdened," Jesus said, "and *I* will give you rest. Take *my* yoke upon you and learn from *me*, for *I* am gentle and humble in heart, and you will find rest for your souls: For *my* yoke is easy and *my* burden is light" (Matthew 11:28–30, emphasis added). No Jewish prophet or teacher ever called people to "come to me." In the Old Testament such promises of refuge and support were offered only to those who would come to the Lord (Isaiah 27:5, 55:3). Jesus obviously viewed himself differently from others who were nurtured in Jewish spirituality.

But as we continue to listen, Jesus goes even further. On a normal Sabbath day at the very beginning of his public ministry, a tiny group gathered in the little synagogue in the town of Nazareth. Coincidentally, or perhaps providentially, the reading from the Scripture that morning was to be from what we know today as Isaiah 61. The scroll was in position and Jesus, who had been attracting attention by teaching in the surrounding area, was invited to read the text and make some comments to those in his hometown. Here is what they heard:

> "The Spirit of the Lord is on me,
> because he has anointed me
> to preach good news to the poor.
> He has sent me to proclaim freedom for the prisoners
> and recovery of sight for the blind,
> to release the oppressed,
> to proclaim the year of the Lord's favor."
> (Luke 4:18–19)

Once seated, as was the custom, Jesus added, "Today this scripture is *fulfilled* in your hearing" (v21, emphasis added). At first, the group, not understanding the import of those words, praised him for his gracious speaking and gushed over him, proud of the local boy who had made good. Having shown him the obligatory courtesies, they were probably ready to go to dinner. But Jesus was not through. Apparently sensing, as he would on many other occasions, that his hearers were not really hearing, Jesus spoke more provocative words. What was particularly disturbing to the people was that he implied that God's love extended to those outside of

Israel. The sleepy synagogue erupted, resulting in Jesus being kicked out of town—not a good day for his mother! It was the first time for her son to preach in his home congregation, and he left everyone more than a little upset.

There are many rich details in this story, but on the surface, it introduces us to an important element in Jesus' self-understanding: *He saw himself as one who was fulfilling Scripture.* Now this was not something you found every day. Had Jesus walked you to the door after dinner at his house and told you that he felt compelled to preach and that he felt he was in the line of the prophets, you might have been surprised, but you would have realized that such feelings were not without precedent. While those ideas might have taken you aback, your knowledge of earlier Biblical history would have told you that God had frequently sent people in such roles. However, to say he was fulfilling past revelation and beginning something God had promised centuries ago, was something altogether different and could be exciting or disturbing, depending on a number of other factors.

What Jesus said in his hometown, he would say in other places. "Do not think that I have come to abolish the Law or the Prophets; I have not come to abolish them but to fulfill them" (Matthew 5:17). The Jews of Jesus' day had always believed the things written in the Law and the Prophets would one day be fulfilled, but by the nation of Israel itself. Yes, there would be a Messiah, but his primary role, according to their expectations, was to lead the nation to the fulfillment of all God's promises. But Jesus says something remarkable. He sees himself as *the one* who will fulfill the revelation that had come earlier from God.

Luke tells us that Jesus predicted his death, insisting it had to happen so that everything written about him in the prophets would be fulfilled (Luke 18:31). A similar passage occurs at the end of Luke's Gospel (Luke 24:25–27). In John's Gospel, Jesus tells the Jews that they should study the Scriptures, but they need to understand that "these are the Scriptures that testify about me" (John 5:39–40). Hundreds of years before he lived, these Old Testament scriptures had been written by the prophets of God. They looked forward to a time when God would bring certain remarkable things to pass. Jesus says, in so many words, "The things you have been reading about for years are being fulfilled through me. God's kingdom is coming and it is coming through me." It was a stunning claim on his part, and one that provoked all kinds of reactions. It surely surprised everyone. For some it was an arrogant and reckless claim. A few dared to hope that it was the good news of a new day.

## Shocking Claims

Having aroused the interest, if not the wrath, of those who knew him, Jesus would go further still. In a story reported early in all except the fourth Gospel, Jesus encounters a man who is paralyzed, and in the course of their conversation tells him that his sins are forgiven. When the Pharisees (members of a prominent sect of the Jews) object to this, charge him with blasphemy and declare that only God can forgive sins, Jesus replies that "the Son of Man has authority on earth to forgive sins" (Mark 2:10). To back up his claim, he heals the man. Thus Jesus introduces the idea that he can take away sin, a claim never before made by any legitimate figure in the history of Israel.

Luke tells us that some time later, Jesus presumes the same authority with regard to a prostitute who intrudes on a private dinner he was having at the home of an inquiring Pharisee (Luke 7:36–50). Her plan was to come in to wash and anoint Jesus' feet. In the presence of the disapproving Pharisee, Jesus assures her that her sins are forgiven and that her faith has saved her. A buzz, of course, is created among the guests. "Who is this who even forgives sins?" (Luke 7:49). In other words, "Who is this man to say things like this?"

All of this set the stage for his more specific claims. In the eighth chapter of John's Gospel, the story is told of another woman who received grace from Jesus after being caught in an adulterous act. This is followed by a conversation apparently with Jewish leaders. "I told you," Jesus says, "that you would die in your sins; if you do not believe that I am the one I claim to be, you will indeed die in your sins" (John 8:24). Clearly, Jesus believed that who he was and what he did was the key to salvation for all people. After influencing a tax collector named Zacchaeus to change his life, Jesus said, "For the Son of Man came to seek and to save what was lost" (Luke 19:10). He clearly saw that he was the one who could forgive sins and bring salvation.

But his clearest statements about this role were made as he came to Jerusalem for the last time. Having just predicted the events that would bring about his death (Mark 10:32–34), Jesus had to intervene in a dispute among his still clueless disciples. Continuing his effort to convince his position-conscious followers that they needed to be servants, not men of power, Jesus made this statement:

> "Whoever wants to become great among you must be your servant, and whoever wants to be first must be slave of all.

> For even the Son of Man did not come to be served, but to serve, and to give his life as a ransom for many." (Mark 10:43–45)

Jesus chose this term "Son of Man" to identify himself on many occasions. It was a name loaded with various meanings for a first century Jew, but one that Jesus used to indicate his unique role in God's plan. We see in this "Son of Man" phrase that Jesus saw himself as the one who would give his life as a ransom "for many." He obviously believed that his death would bring salvation to others. As he ate the last Passover meal with his disciples a short time later, Matthew tells us that "he took the cup, gave thanks and offered it to them, saying, 'Drink from it, all of you. This is my blood of the covenant, which is poured out for many for the forgiveness of sins'" (Matthew 26:27–28). Throughout history men and women have certainly been willing to die for their causes and their convictions, but what sane person up to this point would have ever believed that his death would make the difference in the world's salvation? Jesus obviously had such a conviction.

Few men in the history of religion have identified themselves as the savior of the world and of those who have, Jesus is probably the only one you have ever heard of. The rest were long ago written off as crackpots, maniacs or diabolical deceivers. No religious group in the world today that is treated seriously follows a man who makes such claims, except those who call themselves Christians. The radical claims Jesus made came from deeply held convictions within him. Many who knew him well decided that his life and character fit with these claims. Many still do.

While Jesus saw himself as the one who could save men, he similarly held that judgment was peculiarly in his hands. It is John who reports this saying of Jesus:

> "For as the Father has life in himself, so he has granted the Son to have life in himself. And he has given him authority to judge because he is the Son of Man.
> "Do not be amazed at this, for a time is coming when all who are in their graves will hear his voice and come out— those who have done good will rise to live, and those who have done evil will rise to be condemned. By myself I can do nothing; I judge only as I hear, and my judgment is just, for I seek not to please myself but him who sent me." (John 5:26–30)

Jesus saw himself as the one who would judge, and he was confident about making that judgment because (1) the right to do so had been given to him by God and (2) he was motivated by a desire to please only God with his judgments.

Additionally, the Sermon on the Mount is one of the most powerful statements of ethics ever delivered. Probably no similar statement has been so frequently quoted, and we will later turn our attention to it more specifically. However, it is important to note that in this famous and revered sermon, Jesus is not content to just talk about the type of moral standard we should all live by. He does something a normal preacher or prophet would never do: he talks about his role in judging whether or not the rest of us have lived the way we should.

> "Not everyone who says to me, 'Lord, Lord,' will enter the kingdom of heaven, but only he who does the will of my Father who is in heaven. Many will say to me on that day, 'Lord, Lord, did we not prophesy in your name, and in your name drive out demons and perform many miracles?' Then I will tell them plainly, 'I never knew you. Away from me, you evildoers!'" (Matthew 7:21–23)

Do we understand how incredible it is for a man to talk like this? Here is a person in his early thirties. He doesn't look all that impressive physically (Isaiah 53:2), and he is telling us not only how to live, but that on the last day, we will all be calling him "Lord." He further insists that some of us would do things in his name while our hearts were somewhere else and that as a result, he would have to make the judgment that we cannot enter the kingdom of heaven. What do you do with a man like this? Surely, he is either like none other or he is the most presumptuous man in history.

No genuine prophet of God had ever come and preached that people should be committed to him or that people should love him. The object of one's commitment was to be God, and therefore the prophet's message focused the people—not on himself, but on the God who sent him. Certainly, Jesus sought to draw people to God. Jesus himself openly talked of his dependence on God as in John 5:19, when he says, "I tell you the truth, the Son can do nothing by himself; he can do only what he sees his Father doing, because whatever the Father does the Son also does." And yet, in spite of these humble statements, Jesus called men and women to be personally committed to him.

I don't think we can begin to understand how shocking it would have been to those first century Jews to hear Jesus saying things like the following (emphasis added):

> "Anyone who loves his father or mother more than me is not worthy of me; anyone who loves his son or daughter more than me is not worthy of me; and anyone who does not take his cross and *follow me* is not worthy of me." (Matthew 10:37–38)

> "Whoever finds his life will lose it, and whoever loses his life *for my sake* will find it." (Matthew 10:39)

> "And everyone who has left houses or brothers or sisters or father or mother or children or fields *for my sake* will receive a hundred times as much and will inherit eternal life." (Matthew 19:29)

Surely they thought, "Who is this man? How can he say such things? By what authority does he speak words like these? Didn't he grow up in Nazareth? Don't we know his mother and father and his brothers? How can a man like this ask us all to be totally committed to him and to put him above all those who are near and dear to us?" Today, if anyone talked like Jesus talked, we would rightly start making charges about a cult.

If you have ever thought that Jesus was just a really nice man with a really nice message of love and peace, you must give up that idea. Jesus was the most radical personality ever to live on planet Earth. He clearly taught that the exciting, fulfilling life that God intends for all people comes only to those who make him the object of their devotion. John gives us one of Jesus' clearest statements about this: "I am the way and the truth and the life. No one comes to the Father except through me" (John 14:6).[5]

When it comes to Jesus, any intellectually honest person must take a strong stand—a stand either *for* him or *against* him. His statements do not allow us to straddle the fence. Given what we know he believed about himself, we must either write him off as a crackpot (or a sinister deceiver) or commit ourselves to him wholeheartedly. The people of Jesus' own day got this one right. Some said he ought to die. Others worshiped him as Lord. Those are the choices.

Who do *you* think he was?

# 2

# His Dependence on God

J esus' words force us to make a choice. I am sure you do
not have much trouble figuring out which side I have
come out on. Had I decided that he was a wild-eyed
crackpot or a nasty fraud, I am afraid I would not have found
much inspiration for a book, at least not about him. It is hard
for me to imagine another human being saying what Jesus
said. There are times when the whole story sounds too incredible. Yet the more I have looked at him, the more true I have
decided he is. James Woodroof describes the fact that in Jesus
we are confronted with both "unbelievables" and "undeniables."[1] I must confess that for me the unbelievables are still
there, but the undeniables have won the day. There is simply
too much evidence, too much impact, too much truth and too
much love. I have decided that God did invade this planet in
Jesus. If you are not there yet, keep reading. Let's begin to
look closely at what he was like.

## On God and Not Ourselves

No one ever claimed to be able to do as much as Jesus
claimed he could do—at least no one you would care to follow. And yet at the same time, it is unlikely that any man ever
felt and expressed more dependence on God than Jesus did.
In fact, there is a connection here. His confidence in what he
could do grew out of his understanding of what utter and

complete dependence on God would mean in someone's life. He knew first of all who he was. And secondly, he knew what the results would be if he completely depended on God. From such an understanding flowed an unbounded confidence in what he could accomplish.

For many people the word "dependent" is a word with all kinds of negative connotations. We hear that "Linda is a very dependent person," meaning she is unable to think for herself and has to have someone else telling her what she should do. We hear, "After all these years Ralph is still financially dependent on his parents," and we think that he must be a lazy, good-for-nothing. For the last fourteen years I have lived in New England, and every day I encounter what many call a true Yankee mind-set, going back to the days of the Revolution, in which a person views dependence as a weakness and independence as the greatest of virtues.

Wherever you live in the world and whatever your genetic and environmental background, it is likely that you feel much the same way. However, when it comes to a relationship with God, there is no more positive word than the word "dependence." It may be a hard idea for us to swallow, but the Scriptures consistently teach that real life is found by man when he learns complete dependence on God:

> This is what the LORD says:
>
> "Cursed is the one who trusts in man,
>     who depends on flesh for his strength
>     and whose heart turns away from the LORD....
>
> "But blessed is the man who trusts in the LORD,
>     whose confidence is in him.
> He will be like a tree planted by the water
>     that sends out its roots by the stream."
> (Jeremiah 17:5, 7–8)

> Trust in the LORD with all your heart
>     and lean not on your own understanding.
> (Proverbs 3:5)

The Biblical message says life is not found by depending on ourselves or on the resources of other men, but it is found in dependence on God. Our prideful hearts may not like that at all, but loud denial of our need does not change reality. We are not the self-determined creators of the universe; we are fragile elements of creation. We may wish it were not so, but wishing does not change who and what we are.

However, when we come to Jesus, we might think that since he was not only human but also divine, there would be no need for such a dependence in his case. But apparently, his divine wisdom caused him to see even more clearly how deeply he, as a human, needed to depend on the heavenly Father. His divine nature did not cause him to pridefully conclude, as many of us mere mortals do, that he could make it on his own. It caused him to understand thoroughly that he needed the Father and the Father's help and guidance every day of his life. (If he had such a need, what about us?)

## The Emphasis of the Fourth Gospel

Jesus' dependence on God is there in all the Gospels, but perhaps it is in John that we can see the details of his dependence most clearly. John leaves us little doubt that one of the main ideas Jesus wanted to communicate to his hearers was "I can do nothing on my own—I am totally dependent on the Father."

> Jesus gave them this answer: "I tell you the truth, the Son can do nothing by himself; he can do only what he sees his Father doing, because whatever the Father does the Son also does." (John 5:19)

> "By myself I can do nothing; I judge only as I hear, and my judgment is just, for I seek not to please myself but him who sent me." (John 5:30)

Here is a man who is confident about what he does. Here is a man who will later describe himself as the "I Am" (John 8:58), the good shepherd (John 10:11), the gate (John 10:7), the way, the truth and the life (John 14:6). But in spite of these great claims, he stresses that without a dependence on the Father, he can do nothing. This is just another way in which Jesus is set apart from other men who have made great claims about themselves. Almost always such claims are traceable to arrogant and self-deceived hearts. Not so with Jesus. No one was ever more bold and confident about who he was, and yet no one was ever more humble. But was Jesus just saying this to sound humble? We have good reason to doubt that. What is more likely is that he was convinced to the core of his being that if he tried to do his work and fulfill his purpose without the Father's help he would fail. Notice the following five ways in which Jesus expressed this conviction in John's Gospel:

1.) "I do not have a mission that is my own doing."

> Then Jesus, still teaching in the temple courts, cried out, "Yes, you know me, and you know where I am from. I am not here on my own, but he who sent me is true. You do not know him." (John 7:28)

> Jesus said to them, "If God were your Father, you would love me, for I came from God and now am here. I have not come on my own; but he sent me." (John 8:42)

> "I have brought you glory on earth by completing the work you gave me to do." (John 17:4)

## 2.) "I do not have authority on my own."

"And [God] has given him authority to judge because he is the Son of Man." (John 5:27)

Jesus answered, "My teaching is not my own. It comes from him who sent me.

"If anyone chooses to do God's will, he will find out whether my teaching comes from God or whether I speak on my own. He who speaks on his own does so to gain honor for himself, but he who works for the honor of the one who sent him is a man of truth; there is nothing false about him." (John 7:16–18)

After Jesus said this, he looked toward heaven and prayed:

"Father, the time has come. Glorify your Son, that your Son may glorify you. For you granted him authority over all people that he might give eternal life to all those you have given him." (John 17:1–2)

## 3.) "I cannot draw people to myself on my own."

"All that the Father gives me will come to me, and whoever comes to me I will never drive away." (John 6:37)

"No one can come to me unless the Father who sent me draws him, and I will raise him up at the last day." (John 6:44)

## 4.) "I cannot judge on my own."

"You judge by human standards; I pass judgment on no one. But if I do judge, my decisions are right, because I am not alone. I stand with the Father, who sent me." (John 8:15–16)

## 5.) "I cannot glorify myself."

Jesus replied, "If I glorify myself, my glory means nothing. My Father, whom you claim as your God, is the one who glorifies me." (John 8:54)

Knowing himself to be the preexistent Son of God, the one who was with God and was God, Jesus had to have faced the temptation to think he was capable of handling his life, mission, judgments and tasks on his own; instead he consistently announced his dependence on God. Even on those occasions when he makes bold claims about what he can do, he quickly clarifies where his resources and guidance come from:

> "No one takes it from me, but I lay it down of my own accord. I have authority to lay it down and authority to take it up again. This command I received from my Father." (John 10:18)

Just when it sounds like he might be slipping into a bit of an "I'm operating independently here" attitude, he quickly adds, "This command I received from my Father."

We may sometimes think that Jesus heard the voice of God and knew the will of God more clearly because he was the Son of God. While this sounds reasonable, it is not exactly what we read in the Gospel of John. "He who belongs to God hears what God says. The reason you do not hear is that you do not belong to God" (John 8:47). "Belong" here certainly carries with it the idea of "depends on." Jesus heard the voice of God so clearly because he so clearly understood himself to be a person who was dependent on God. In every way he was not on his own, but he "belonged" to God.

I hope you find all of this interesting, but I hope it is more than interesting to you. I hope you remember that we are concerned in this book about the whole issue of learning how to live. I hope you have in mind that we are looking at Jesus so that he might train us for living. The five points above are not just interesting facts about Jesus; they are guideposts for our lives.

I do not have a mission of my own doing, and I cannot generate an eternally meaningful mission on my own. If I want to find out what my purpose in life is, I need to submit to the mission God has perfectly designed for me. (More on this later in the book.)

I do not have authority on my own and cannot judge on my own what is right and what is wrong. If I try, my subjectivity and emotions will certainly get in the way. I cannot independently decide what should be praised and what should be condemned. I must instead listen to the truth God has revealed through his prophets, apostles and most of all, through his Son.

I cannot attract people to the gospel message on my own. Sure, if I have certain gifts of speech and charisma, I may be able to draw people to myself, but I cannot draw people to the truth of God on my own. Even if I decide to be about the mission of God, I must not think that through the clever use of my talents I will be the one who saves the world and brings people to God. The challenge of drawing people to God is so great that it can only be accomplished through dependence on God's power.

Finally, I cannot bring to myself any unfading glory. On my own I may be able to bask for a while in the glory of men, but "all men are like grass and their glory like the flowers of the field; the grass withers and the flowers fall" (Isaiah 40:6–8, quoted also in 1 Peter 1:24–25). While depending on myself, I cannot bring lasting glory to myself, because I certainly cannot bring glory to God.

## The Role of Prayer

While John describes Jesus' conviction about his need for God, Luke in his Gospel shows how this was practically expressed through prayer.

> Yet the news about him spread all the more, so that crowds of people came to hear him and to be healed of their sicknesses. But Jesus often withdrew to lonely places and prayed. (Luke 5:15–16)

As Jesus became a crowd favorite, he did not bask in popularity or take a vacation to celebrate self-sufficiency. No, he pulled away from the accolades to pray to his Father. This text is important because it clearly shows us that Jesus' prayer life and dependence on God was not just centered around periods of crisis, but was something he did "often," as a regular aspect of his life.

In the next chapter of Luke we read:

> One of those days Jesus went out to a mountainside to pray, and spent the night praying to God. When morning came, he called his disciples to him and chose twelve of them, whom he also designated apostles. (Luke 6:12–13)

Prayer to God was not a ritual to do before meals. Jesus saw it as something so essential that he was willing to give up an entire night of sleep to do it before making a major decision. As Jesus got ready to train men, he knew he needed to spend an entire night in prayer drawing close to God and depending totally on him. It is not difficult to argue that Jesus always did what was best, and he knew prayer was what was best and most needful.

Charles Edward Jefferson described the impact that Jesus' prayer life and reliance on God had on those around him:

Men gathered round him awestruck and said, "Master, teach us how to pray." All Hebrew children were taught to pray from earliest infancy. Prayer was an indispensable feature of Hebrew piety, but men who had prayed from earliest youth felt, when they heard this man pray, that they had never prayed at all.[2]

The references to prayer continue in other passages (see Luke 9:18, 28; 11:1 and Mark 1:35). All this emphasis led G. S. S. Thomson to write: "Prayer was the atmosphere in which Jesus lived. It was the air he breathed."[3] Several of Robert Coleman's reflections on Jesus' prayer life are memorable and poignant:

Prayer shines through the gospels like a dominant color in a painting, giving the whole picture a characteristic hue.

Prayer was indeed the sweat and tears of his ministry. The battle of the cross was fought and won on his knees.

Jesus never got behind in his work, because he never got behind in his prayer.[4]

Prayer was the well Jesus went to again and again to gain the needed strength to stay the course and finish the work. Coleman goes on to observe, "Prayer was more important than eating or sleeping. He could get along for periods without either of those, but he could not get along without prayer."[5]

We must not leave our discussion of Jesus' dependence on God without talking about his use of a most interesting word to refer to God as his Father. It was the Aramaic word *Abba*. The use of the word as a term for God was so unique that Mark did not translate it into Greek in Mark 14:36, and Paul used it along with the normal Greek word for "father" in Romans 8:15

and Galatians 4:6. The Biblical writers obviously wanted to make a special point to their Greek-speaking audience. It appears untranslated still in most English versions in these three passages to make the same point for us.

No one has studied this phenomenon more carefully than New Testament scholar Joachim Jeremias. His excruciatingly detailed research brought him to this conclusion: "To date no one has produced one single instance in Palestinian Judaism where God is addressed as 'my Father' by an individual person." He goes on to point out that nowhere in the abundant literature of ancient Judaism is there a single time when God is referred to as *Abba*.[6] "It was the babbling sound," says Andrew Greely, "that a Jewish infant used toward his father, the equivalent of 'dada.' But it was more than that. Grown-up sons and daughters called their fathers *Abba* as well, but only in the context of the greatest tenderness and familiarity."[7] Jeremias concludes that for Jesus to use this term to address God is "something new, something unique, and something unheard of."[8] Jeremias is convinced that this one word alone speaks volumes about Jesus and his message. Certainly, it shows that Jesus felt something in his relationship with God that no Jew had ever documented before. "To the Jewish mind," Jeremias says, "it would have been irreverent and therefore unthinkable to call God by such a familiar word."[9]

By using this simple word, Jesus gives the world a dramatic new way to think of God, shows himself unashamed to be as a child with his Father and opens the door for all of us to enjoy the same kind of intimacy. Several decades later, Paul was still telling Christians (many of whom did not speak a word of Aramaic) that by the power of the Holy Spirit they, too, should cry *"Abba."* This is a clear indication of how revolutionary and powerful this message was—and one the early church did not want to lose.

All we have examined leads to one conclusion: Jesus truly believed that "by myself I can do nothing." But because he came to do something of the greatest importance, he would live each day in dependence on his Father—his *Abba*—for whom nothing was impossible (Mark 10:27).

The overriding key to Jesus' effectiveness as a great and powerful servant of God can be traced to one place. It was not found in his intelligence, his charisma, his talent or even his miraculous powers. It was found in his absolute, unwavering dependence on God. We mistakenly think that Jesus had some incredible advantage over us. But the truth is that he could not do it on his own any more than we can do it on our own. *And what he had going for him, every one of us can have going for us.* What an amazing thought! How will it change us?

# His Servant Heart

J esus is remarkable. We have already seen that he made claims about himself that would be treated as preposterous if most men made them—which is just what his critics thought of them. Once you consider those claims, it seems almost impossible that a person like that could at the same time be considered a man of great humility and the standard-bearer and model of servanthood, but this is exactly what we find when we come to Jesus.

The paradoxical Jesus made great claims about himself, but was not boastful or arrogant. Thomas Olbricht, in a book about the Gospel of Mark, spends an entire chapter on the fact that Jesus was *unassuming* (and by the way, makes a very strong case for this).[1] Olbricht talks about how Jesus did not seek the headlines, the glitter or the recognition for which most men hunger. He notes that Jesus was not concerned about people catering to his every whim, but rather was concerned about being a servant. It is this decision, Jesus' decision to be a servant, that we will examine in this chapter. This was not a position he was in by virtue of a wimpy personality or weak character, but by virtue of strong convictions about how to find life. For some of us, this chapter will challenge to the core our most deep-rooted perceptions about how to "make it" in this world.

Following the 1990 crisis in the Persian Gulf, we heard reports that most of the people of Kuwait, before Iraq's invasion, had servants in their homes (brought in from Third World countries) to take care of their every need. Friends of ours who live in Saudi Arabia report much the same thing there. I suspect this is something you find throughout the oil-rich Gulf states. Most Westerners wish they had it so good. Most people dream of the day when someone will serve them. At the same time, most people see the life of a servant as a life to avoid. Happiness and servanthood hardly seem as if they could coexist. But Jesus' life says clearly: the way to live life for all it is worth is to become a servant.

## His Birth

> So Joseph also went up from the town of Nazareth in Galilee to Judea, to Bethlehem the town of David, because he belonged to the house and line of David. He went there to register with Mary, who was pledged to be married to him and was expecting a child. While they were there, the time came for the baby to be born, and she gave birth to her firstborn, a son. She wrapped him in cloths and placed him in a manger, because there was no room for them in the inn. (Luke 2:4–7)

Ordinarily, the circumstances of a person's birth tell us nothing significant about the character of the person being born. They might on occasion tell us something about the character of the child's parents, but certainly not the child himself. However, in the case of Jesus, the birth story seems to send a strong message about the style of life he would have and is a foreshadowing of things to come.

Because we know the end of the story, the image here is powerful: the preexistent Son of God, the one who fine-tuned the universe, being *born*, and then placed in a feed trough that substitutes for a crib. The one who can do anything he wants whenever he wants to is wrapped in torn strips of cloth and placed in a manger, with no Fisher-Price toys anywhere in sight.

Had Jesus been born in the inn instead of in a place with animals, would that tell us something very different about his character? Not really. In either case, we are talking about an incredible step down. How would you react if you heard the British royals were moving out of Buckingham Palace into a one-room shanty with a wood-burning stove? What would the tabloids do with that? People would be shocked and amazed. It would be on the cover of *People* and probably a few dozen other publications. Everyone would want to know why. However, what we see in the Incarnation was something far more dramatic. In Jesus' case, just the act of being born, when nothing required him to do so, makes quite a statement. But the fact that he entered the world in a stable highlights the point that he was willing to go to the absolute lowest of positions. What followed in the next three decades demonstrated that this was no publicity stunt, but rather an expression of his character. His venture into the low position was neither short-lived nor calculated for effect. It was a demonstration of deep conviction.

## His Mind-Set

Many scholars believe that one of the earliest and most popular Christian hymns is quoted by Paul in Philippians 2. Having told the Philippian disciples, "Your attitude [or mind-set] should be the same as that of Christ Jesus," Paul then quotes this supposed hymn to Christ which would have most

likely been sung in the chant-like form common in the early
church:

> Who, being in very nature God,
>     did not consider equality with God something
>         to be grasped,
> but made himself nothing,
>     taking the very nature of a servant,
>     being made in human likeness.
> And being found in appearance as a man,
>     he humbled himself
>     and became obedient to death—
>         even death on a cross! (Philippians 2:5–8)

What is important about this hymn is that it captures the
church's understanding of Jesus' mind-set at a very early date,
an understanding that no doubt had been passed on by the
apostles and others who had seen it lived out as they walked
the roads of Galilee and Judea—with Jesus in the flesh.

Verse 5 more literally reads, "Have in you this mind that
was also in Christ Jesus." Servanthood was a mind-set for
Jesus. As he lived each day, his mind was set—not on how
much he could gain, not on how much power he could
accumulate, not on who he could impress, and not on how
independent he could become, but on whom he could serve
and how he could best serve them. This is servanthood at its
best. Not an attitude of, "Oh, yes, I do need to squeeze in
some serving today," but minds set on serving in all the
situations we find ourselves in throughout the day. As we saw
in another context, back in chapter 1, Jesus said this to
address the disciples petty squabbling over who would get
top cabinet positions in the kingdom:

> "Whoever wants to become great among you must be your
> servant, and whoever wants to be first must be slave of all.

For even the Son of Man did not come to be served, but to serve, and to give his life as a ransom for many." (Mark 10:43–45)

Jesus looked at why he was here and his conclusion was "I am here to serve." The new Israel, the new people of God, the church he came to build could only be the light of the world if the leaders first understood that their Leader was a servant and that they too must have the mind-set of being servants—yes, even slaves of all. Commenting on Jesus' rebuke of Peter in Mark 8, C. H. Dodd says that when Jesus told Peter he was thinking as men think, not as God thinks, he was saying to Peter, "Your Messiah is a conqueror. God's Messiah is a servant."[2]

Matthew in 12:18–21 quotes from Isaiah 42, one of the first chapters in Isaiah that introduce what are now called the Songs of the Suffering Servant (Isaiah 40–66). There is little doubt that Jesus was shaped and directed by what was written in these songs.[3] The Jews, including Jesus' disciples, were looking for a national liberator who would bring political and social salvation by exercising force and "exorcising" the foreign demons. With this in mind they found very little in the servant songs to attract them. Suffering and serving were not on their wish list. However, Jesus was on a different track. He understood that life is found, not by those who overpower, but by those who serve. He wanted to introduce people to the blessings of the kingdom of God and teach them that the greatest is he who serves.

Sometimes, we talk about the young woman who has her mind set on being a doctor, or the young pitcher who has his mind set on going into the major leagues or the gold medal winner who has his mind set on making a comeback after years of retirement. Maybe for some of us we have our minds set on a certain car or house or on a tropical cruise. Maybe for some their mind is set on rising to a certain position in the kingdom. It would not be the first time a leader was tempted to think this way. But what was Jesus' mind set on? Serving. His focus was not on "What can I get?" but on "What I can give?" And in his mind there did not seem to be even a tinge of legalistic thinking, with its attendant drudgery. There was no "Come on, we have to serve if we want to go to heaven." He was free to serve and free to enjoy serving. We can almost feel this when he washes the disciples' feet in John 13.

With a mind set on serving, there were other things his mind was not set on, and being comfortable was one of those things. If your mind is set on comfort, there will be opportunities to serve that you will pass up because you will fear that your comfort may be disturbed. Jesus certainly would have passed up his most important works of service had this been his mind-set. In a similar way, we cannot have our minds set on serving and at the same time set on looking good. (No one can accuse Jesus of this one!) In such cases, our willingness to serve will be at the mercy of someone else's opinion of how being a servant makes us look. Jesus ignored what others thought in favor of a commitment to serve, regardless of what kind of reviews he received.

*The amazing thing here is that Jesus fundamentally thought of himself as a servant.* He did not, like so many leaders, both religious and secular, see himself as a dignitary who needed to do some acts of service to maintain credibility with the people. He saw himself as a servant who needed to lead others to be servants as well. A servant is one who is present to meet the needs of others, and this is the rudimentary role Jesus took for himself. His philosophy was, "I am not here for myself, to see how much I can get out of all this. I am here for others." Talk about a mind-set that can transform churches, marriages, families, neighborhoods and workplaces—this is it!

Whether he was describing himself as the good shepherd (John 10:11), the living bread (John 6:51), or the great physician (Matthew 9:12), Jesus saw himself as the one who was here on Earth to meet needs. He was not here to earn so much money each year, have the latest model chariot, or get pampered (at least on his birthday). He was the one who was here to meet vital needs in the lives of others. This is a challenge to us all because our minds are forever going back to ourselves and "What is in it for me?" The writing of this book was an effort inspired by my appreciation for Jesus and by my desire for others to be moved, by his incredible qualities, to change. And yet, once in a while as I wrote, I would find myself thinking about what others might think of my work and whether or not it would be praised. As disgusting as this is to me, it reflects a very human tendency that all of us must struggle to overcome. In Jesus we have a model of one who *did* overcome and set his mind not on himself, but on others. By the grace of God, you and I can learn to do the same.

Just one caveat: I do not think most of us are in any danger here, but be careful that you do not start with this and run off to some ascetic extreme. What has been said in this chapter does not mean Jesus never enjoyed anything, never had a great time and never ate anything that tasted "almost as good as heaven." There are clear indications that Jesus enjoyed food with the best of them, and I expect he gave some great compliments to more than one person who prepared a fabulous meal for him. Jesus enjoyed life! Paul would later speak of "God, who richly provides us with everything for our enjoyment" (1 Timothy 6:17). I doubt Paul learned this as a Pharisee. It sounds to me like something that made its way down from Jesus. The servant is no stick in the mud. The servant can joyfully receive—it's just that he is not primarily here to get, but to give.

## Slave of All

Looking back to the passage in Philippians 2, we read in verse 6 a line that can be more accurately translated "being in his very essence God, he did not consider equality with God something to be grasped." Jesus had equality with God. What a thought! He was in his very essence God. But he did not grasp it and cling to it as his prerogative, his right. He was ever so willing to give it up for the benefit of others, and this is perhaps the most staggering idea in the Bible.

Do you have something that you consider more precious than anything else in your life? For Jesus this was his place beside the Father (in a relationship we cannot begin to understand). But Jesus did not hold onto that because grasping it would have meant that there would have been no hope for any of the rest of us to get there. Perhaps the reason Jesus did not have a major struggle with some of the things that trouble us the most is that prior to coming, he had already made the biggest decision: to let go of his place and privileges with the Father. Being a servant means no grasping, no holding on, no trying to save what is ours. It means an end to the protective way of thinking. It means a mind that is set on serving others whatever the cost or discomfort. And yet, it was not with a grim-faced spirit of resignation that Jesus did this, but with a spirit of joy and peace and celebration.

In Matthew 27:41–42, we find an ironic statement by the religious authorities who mocked Jesus at his crucifixion: "He saved others," they said, "but he can't save himself! He's the King of Israel! Let him come down now from the cross, and we will believe in him." But there was something they missed: "What they failed to understand," writes Robert Coleman, "is that Jesus was not in the world to save himself. He was here to save us. No one can finally save himself and still fulfill the mission of God."[4]

This is all closely intertwined with the statement in that early hymn recorded in Philippians 2:7. Translated in the New International Version as "he made himself nothing" it is more accurately rendered "he emptied himself" (from the Greek verb *keneo*). Theologians have debated for centuries the exact meaning of this concept. Did Jesus empty himself of all of his past understanding of God from his preexistence? Did he give up all of his supernatural knowledge? Yet, to get bogged down in a theological debate here is to miss the point. In the context, he emptied himself of his prerogatives and privileges. He emptied himself of his right to be served, and translating the text more literally yields: "he became in his *essence* a bondservant" (or a slave—*doulos* in Greek). He had all rights but he was willing, for the sake of others, to live as though he had none. A bondservant was a man with no personal rights, as one of Jesus' own stories clearly illustrated:

> "Suppose one of you had a servant plowing or looking after the sheep. Would he say to the servant when he comes in from the field, 'Come along now and sit down to eat'? Would he not rather say, 'Prepare my supper, get yourself ready and wait on me while I eat and drink; after that you may eat and drink'? Would he thank the servant because he did what he was told to do? So you also, when you have

done everything you were told to do, should say, 'We are unworthy servants; we have only done our duty.'" (Luke 17:7–10)

It was this mind-set that Jesus chose to have for himself—the mind-set of one who did not think in terms of his rights, but rather in terms of his responsibilities. Jesus told his disciples that they had to become slaves of all (Mark 10:44), which is exactly what this great hymn to Jesus declares that he did become. Jesus did not just expect this of others—he lived it first. Slaves have responsibilities, but not rights.

I know this concept challenges us to the core of our being. We naturally think in terms of our rights. In many situations, this is our first reaction. We can think of our right to be treated fairly and our right to get a decent night's sleep and our right to decide how we want to use our Saturday after-noons and our right to some fun after a hard period of work…and on and on we could go. In fact, there is nothing wrong with getting any of these things, but our preoccupation with our "rights" keeps us from serving. Such a focus also brings us into conflict with others who are fighting to protect their own rights. What Jesus is trying to retrain us to do is to "empty ourselves" of all these rights and, in the spirit of the bondservant, to take up our responsibilities.

I will speak frankly here. If it were not for the example of Jesus and the outcome of his way of life, I would never buy into such a philosophy. It sounds too risky. It sounds like I am going to give up everything and be left with nothing. It sounds like I will be dangerously close to becoming the door-mat of the world to be walked on by everyone. Instinctively, I wonder, "If I become the slave of all, who will end up taking care of me? Will I be left as a worn-out, used and abused fellow who misses all the fun, while others who protect their rights get the good things in life?" I am confident that as you look at Jesus' life and message, these thoughts occur to you as well.

The answer to our concerns, of course, lies in the paradox that when we give up all that "What's going to happen to me?" stuff, God sees to it that some great things do happen to us. In changing our hearts, we become so in tune with his mindset and heart that his blessings flow into our lives. In addition, God has so arranged things that when we fulfill our responsibilities to others with a joyful heart that is grateful to be able to give, we find ourselves plugged into situations that can give us the greatest joy.

Jesus boldly lived as a servant and, without the slightest hesitation, called his disciples to be servants as well. His deep conviction was that "whoever tries to keep his life will lose it, and whoever loses his life will preserve it" (Luke 17:33). The hymn found in Philippians 2 concludes with an assurance that he was not disappointed:

> Therefore God exalted him to the highest place
> and gave him the name that is above every name,
> that at the name of Jesus every knee should bow,
> in heaven and on earth and under the earth,
> and every tongue confess that Jesus Christ is Lord,
> to the glory of God the Father. (Philippians 2:9–11)

In Jesus, we really do learn that it is more blessed to give than to receive. Are you, because of trust in Jesus and his message, ready to lose your life and take the form of a servant?

# Rich in Character

**A** very special friend of mine died suddenly and quite shockingly just a few months ago. I was not able to travel to the West Coast for his memorial service, but a few weeks later I received a videotape of it. As I listened to a number of people share about him, I was moved to tears more than once. They described aspects of his character that I remembered so well, and they shared a few fun and moving stories about him that I had not heard, but knowing him, could easily imagine. We all were touched by the memory of his character. Who we really are is not so much about the job we have or the role we play as it is about the qualities of our *character* that others around us experience.

The term "character" can be used to refer to the complex combination of traits that distinguishes an individual. In this chapter we are concerned about the qualities and traits of Jesus that most distinguish his life. Had he simply been a man who made some outrageous claims about himself, it is doubtful that you and I would have ever heard of him. But along with those claims and the miracles he performed came a life and a lifestyle that attracted the attention of people. In the two previous chapters we have looked at Jesus' reliance on God and his servant attitude. Both were integral to his personhood, but of course there was more. Let's start with the unexpected.

## His Submissiveness

Seldom in books on Jesus will you find submissiveness mentioned as one of the aspects of his personality and character, probably because it is viewed by many as a weak and wimpy quality, not as a strength. Consequently, few are really looking for it in Jesus. But submissiveness is one of the most misunderstood ideas and most underrated qualities. We misunderstand what it is and we certainly misunderstand what a powerful principle it is in the plan of God—and even in the character of God himself.

Some time ago, when I began studying the Gospel of Mark in search of the character and personality of Jesus, submissiveness was the first thing I wrote down about him. We do not go much more than two paragraphs into that Gospel before we read of Jesus submitting to John the Baptist via his baptism in the Jordan River (Mark 1:4–9). Jesus clearly understood his vital role in God's plan. He would soon be preaching that he was the fulfillment of the Scriptures. John was simply a prophet sent before him to prepare the way for him. John was not fit to carry the sandals of Jesus, and he admitted as much. And yet Jesus came out, and no doubt lined up with the rest of the people and humbly submitted himself to John's baptism.

While living in another state years ago, Sheila and I were in the process of selling our home to a man who just happened to work as the head of a state welfare office. In order to get his signature on a document, I had to go to the place where he worked. When I arrived there, I went to a security guard and told him of my desire to see this gentleman. I was told by the guard that I would have to stand in line with others who were waiting there to see him. I looked around at the poor of our community, all waiting with rather empty expressions to see this man who would make some decision about the money they would receive. Something in me rebelled. I did not want to stand there and look like I was waiting for a handout. I did not want to be identified with those people. I wanted special treatment because I was someone else and had other business.

But then in that moment, as I stood there in that cold, institutional waiting room, I thought of Jesus going out to John the Baptist to be baptized. John was preaching a baptism of repentance for the forgiveness of sins and it was understood that those who were coming were sinners in need of forgiveness. They were standing in line waiting for John in order that they might receive something from him they could not do for themselves. Jesus could have felt as I felt that day in the welfare agency. He could have said, "I don't have to be here because I'm different," but he came and submitted to the man God had sent.

In Matthew's Gospel we read that John himself had serious questions about whether this ought to happen. "I need to be baptized by you," said John, "and do you come to me?" (Matthew 3:14). Jesus replied, "It is proper to do this to fulfill all righteousness" (v15). Tragically, many have understood this to mean that "baptism is one of the requirements, and I need to be sure I have checked off all the requirements, so go ahead and baptize me." I, however, am convinced that Jesus meant much more by his statement. Being deeply submissive to the will of God and to the people God puts in our lives is one of the great keys to righteousness. Here Jesus saw that it was essential that he too submit to the prophet of God, the divine forerunner, and in so doing, get on a track that would lead to an even more profound submission. Never mind that Jesus was greater than the one he was submitting to. Similarly, there are times in our lives when God puts us under the authority of someone else. By various measurements we may be "greater" than they are, but these situations become tests of our hearts. Jesus passed the test, showing not a prideful and arrogant spirit, but a submissive one. He was secure in who he was, and his confidence and his security in his identity left him free to be submissive—even when it could have made him look like something he was not.

For argument's sake let's say that it is not all that challenging to be submissive to a humble and good man like John, even when you are greater than he is. However, at the end of the Gospels we see Jesus submitting to different kinds of men altogether. At the conclusion of his life, we find Jesus still submitting to the will of God, but this time, ironically, God uses some men who are self-centered and arrogant, both religious and irreligious. Jesus submitted to the cross at the hands of men who were unrighteous and haughty. His trait of submissiveness was present, regardless of who was "over" him at the moment. We should be quick to note that it was not cowardice or weakness of will that led Jesus to submit to the cross and "open not his mouth" (Isaiah 53:7 KJV). It was his conviction that God was at work in this and that lives would be won by his submission to the plan of God—no matter how obnoxious or conceited were the people to whom he was submitting.

Lest you think I am making too much of this quality, do some careful study of the letter of 1 Peter, and see a man who knew Jesus well and eventually got the point Jesus was making. Certainly, no one initially had more problems with submission than Peter, but in his letter he holds it out as a mighty principle of life. Jesus is set forth as the one who shows us the way to live submissively, in order that we might follow in his steps (see 1 Peter 2:21 as it appears in the context of 2:13–25). After many years Peter learned that submissiveness is no third-rate quality, but one that needs to be seen in all disciples as it was seen so clearly in Jesus.

## His Courage

While it may be surprising to speak of the submissiveness of a great man, we expect to see boldness and courage in the lives of those who have great impact, and we are not disappointed when we come to Jesus. Submissive—yes. Timid and fearful—absolutely not. It is this combination of qualities that we find hard to understand or implement, but which makes Jesus so unique and worthy of imitation.

Jesus' courage is seen first in the way he challenged the masses who followed him. While he viewed them as "harassed and helpless, like sheep without a shepherd" (Matthew 9:36), he never dealt with them sentimentally. If they wanted to follow him, they would have to deny themselves and take up a cross. He had none of the normal political instincts or concerns for popularity and showed no fear of losing followers over strong words. Luke says that "large crowds were traveling with Jesus" when he spoke dramatically of giving loyalty to himself above any loyalty to family or loved ones (Luke 14:25–27). To that same crowd he issued his challenge to count the cost and realize that there could be no discipleship and thus no salvation for those who were unwilling to give up everything (vv28–33).

In the wake of these and other strong words, John tells us that there were some who reacted and said, "This is a hard teaching. Who can accept it?" (John 6:60), and later he reports, "From this time many of his disciples turned back and no longer followed him" (v66). Even in the face of massive defections, Jesus did not change his message. Jesus was not out to be popular. He hated to see people leave, because he knew they were turning from life, but he would not run after them with a message of compromise. A person's decision to be with him needed to be based on a full understanding of the truth, however challenging that truth might be to their character, traditions and lifestyle. The rich young ruler saw this side of Jesus clearly and learned first hand that Jesus would adjust his message for no one, regardless of how impressive, religious or influential he might be (see Luke 18:18–30).

Jesus' courage is seen second in his confrontations with the religious leaders of his day (an important issue we will look at carefully in chapter 11). An intimidating group, they had power, position and prestige. He had none of these from a human perspective. He came from the wrong town, had no educational credentials, and his lieutenants were more common and unlearned than he was. But once again, because of his unshakable confidence in his own identity and mission, he never missed a chance to challenge hypocrisy, duplicity and the self-serving hearts of those who should have been providing spiritual direction for the masses. Submissiveness as a character trait did not mean silence or cowardice. It meant courageously giving up self for the good of others, neither holding back the message that others needed to hear nor failing to expose darkness for what it was. Jesus never held back.

He thoroughly critiqued the religious establishment, exposing their false motives, inconsistencies, hypocritical positions and negative effects on others (see Matthew 23:1–36). He minced no words, calling them "blind guides, whitewashed tombs and a brood of vipers." But these challenges were not issued from afar. He marched in on their turf, into the temple itself, where they ruled the roost, and he turned over their money-changing (and money-making) tables, driving them out with sharp words of rebuke about turning a house of prayer into a den of robbers. It is of little wonder that the Jewish Council would later see the courage of Peter and John after the resurrection of Jesus and conclude (but not happily) that those men had been with Jesus (Acts 4:13). They saw in these disciples the same spirit they had hoped to be rid of.

Third, Jesus' courage is seen in his determination to go to the cross. Have you ever set your mind and walked into a situation, knowing full well the opposition or retaliation that awaited you? It gives one pause. Jesus fully understood the implications of going to Jerusalem the last time. He knew the prophecies. He knew the treatment he would receive. He knew the kind of death he would die, but Luke 9:51 says he "resolutely set out for Jerusalem." One of the most memorable comments I have ever heard about Jesus was made in reflection on this verse: "Jesus leaned into his pain." And in so doing—what a model he is for us. It is at this point that we see his submissiveness and his courage so completely bound together, for it often takes the highest level of courage to be submissive to the will of God. He understood that he not only would suffer physically in Jerusalem but that there would also be the suffering of his soul as one totally separated from God for the sins of others. But convinced of who he was and what his purpose was, and convinced of ultimate vindication from

God, he "set his face like flint" (Isaiah 50:7) and headed for Jerusalem. He had his fears, but his courage overcame them.

## His Compassion and Love

Often those who go out heroically and fight the windmills of wrong do not show much interest in the less glamorous situations in which someone needs a caring touch. But this was not the case with Jesus. He was the original man of steel and velvet. One minute he was boldly marching in to cleanse the temple of corruption, while the next, he was giving his total attention to some poor woman who had been sick for many years. Such events as these were not staged by some PR man to look good on the evening news; they were a part of his life, day in and day out.

Reading through the Gospel of Mark, I am immediately impressed with how often Jesus was in those situations of touching and caring. It may have kept him up late into the night, but he kept giving (1:29–34). It may have involved touching the untouchables, but Jesus was willing (1:40–41). It may have even meant accusations about wrong associations, but Jesus came to show compassion to those who needed a doctor, not to spend his time with those who thought they were already healthy and didn't need a thing (Luke 5:31).

When women feel comfortable bringing their children to a strong leader, it says something very significant about him. Now, this bothered his more macho disciples, but Jesus felt totally comfortable with it, and apparently these mothers felt from him that he would welcome their small children (Matthew 19:13–15). Such interactions are real indicators of the common touch that Jesus had and the compassion and concern that people could sense from his life.

# His Joy

I was once involved in working on an issue of a magazine that was devoted entirely to Jesus. One of the articles dealt with the distortions of Jesus through the centuries and was illustrated with artwork depicting him, created mostly in the first 1,000 years of church history. Not one of the pictures or statues we could find depicted what you would call a happy or a joyful Jesus. They were all rather glum-looking fellows. And that, in fact, is most people's view of Jesus. Isaiah was right, of course, when he prophesied that Jesus would be a man of sorrows, acquainted with grief (Isaiah 53:3). He did carry a heavy burden and had some moments of great distress and intense anguish, but this is not the whole story.

In spite of all the responsibility he felt and all the suffering he knew would be his, Jesus never fell into bitterness, negative thinking or despair. His outlook and expectations were positive. He may not have had something funny to say in every situation, although some of the stories he told show a definite sense of humor, but he consistently emphasized the positive. "Yes," he said, "in this world you will have trouble [it will come—you can count on it]. But take heart! ['Cheer up!' one version says.] I have overcome the world" (John 16:33).

Jesus believed that you can feel joyful about life even when you are taking some hard hits from the forces of evil. In the final analysis God is going to win, and this confidence permeated his spirit. We can see it in the many encouraging words, laced with joy, that he spoke on the night he knew would be his last. He told his disciples that he wanted to leave them with his peace, the very peace that had guarded his own heart (John 14:27). He talked to them specifically about the complete joy that they could have as they implemented his teachings and drew near to God (John 16:21–24).

Jesus was a joyful person, and he trained others to have the same joy that he had. Yes, he was intense. Yes, he was dead serious about sin in people's lives and abuses in religion, but his communion with God and awareness of how God was working was enough to give him a glad heart. For those who loved God, the end was going to be good. And so the writer of Hebrews tells us that Jesus "for the joy set before him endured the cross, scorning its shame, and sat down at the right hand of the throne of God" (Hebrews 12:2). Life is tough, but life with God is better, and for those who love him, God wins out. Therefore, joy makes sense.

The Gospels describe a Jesus who goes to weddings and banquets and who often uses such events in his parables. As we said in the last chapter, he was a man who enjoyed life. Some of his critics found this quite unacceptable and accused him of having too good a time—being in their eyes a glutton, a drunkard and a comrade of sinners (Matthew 11:19). Like so many before and since, these religious leaders had come to associate loyalty to God with a long face and spirituality with a stern set of the jaw. This was just one of their traditions that Jesus rejected. He not only enjoyed his food, his friends and the goodness of life here, but he saw heaven itself as a joyous feast (Matthew 8:10–11).

## His Balance

There is not space here to describe all the aspects of Jesus' character and personality.[1] What can be said in summary is that there is an amazing balance in him. Somewhere I came across this well-put statement: "Jesus is tender without being weak, strong without being coarse, lowly without being servile. He has conviction without intolerance, enthusiasm without fanaticism, holiness without Pharisaism, passion without prejudice." I would add to this that Jesus was purposeful, but unhurried. He was consistent without being legalistic. He was determined, but not tense. He was loving, but not sentimental.

We must be careful when we look at Jesus to not be simply awestruck. Here is the man who is showing us how to live, and amazingly, what we see in him can be seen in us in ever-increasing measure as we enroll in his school of discipleship. In Jesus we see the character of God, but we also see the character that man was meant to have when originally created in the image of God.

As we look at Jesus' character and seek to find for our own lives how to really live, we must not pick and choose traits. We must not select his courage, but reject his submissiveness. We must not choose his joy, but reject his compassion for others. To find life ourselves, we must begin by submitting to the character of Jesus, wanting not part of him but all of him to be impressed on our inner being. Such an undertaking will require an infusion of God's grace into our lives. But the struggle to become like him is well worth it, for there really is no one like him.

# Jesus and the Scriptures

I recently spent many hours over a period of months with a good friend who was considering becoming a disciple of Jesus. Much to my delight, he has since made that decision. However, surrounded by a culture that often questions, sometimes ridicules and most regularly dismisses the Bible, he wrestled for a long time with the Scriptures. He was drawn by the basic message. He felt a deep need for God. He believed in Jesus. But he didn't know if he could wholeheartedly embrace the Scriptures.

I quite candidly shared with him that after more than thirty years of Scripture study, I still found questions I could not answer and passages that either confused me or troubled me, but I told him that nothing had been more helpful to me than to carefully consider Jesus' view of the Scriptures. Although most books about Jesus that I have seen do not explore this area, it is a vital one, with huge implications. We are looking in these first few chapters at what kind of man Jesus was, the kinds of things that were most true of him. This will require that we look at his view of the Scriptures and his source of authority.

A portion of our Bible (about a third of it) was written after the life of Jesus to bear witness to his life and explain his message. This, of course, is what we call the New Testament. But an even larger portion of the Scriptures were already in existence during Jesus' time. If he was in fact the one he claimed to be, it is most important to know how he viewed these Scriptures. Here are some possibilities:

- Did he view them simply as human literature, as man's reflections about life and God?
- Did he view them as significant, but often erroneous and sometimes misleading, writings?
- Did he view them as important and correct writings that would need to be supplemented by human traditions?
- Or did he see the Scriptures as the authoritative word of God that must be relied on and obeyed?

These questions are important for an obvious reason: We are in this study to be trained or discipled by Jesus. Once we see what Jesus' view of the Scriptures was, then we will know what our view should be.

Jesus had open to him all the options that we just mentioned. He could have taken any of these viewpoints. Some have argued that Jesus was a child of his culture and just accepted whatever his culture taught about these things. Say what you want about Jesus—if you choose, call him a drunkard or a glutton, as some did in his day, but do not say he was one who merely conformed to his cultural norms. Among other things, he did not accept his culture's view of Samaritans, Gentiles, women, lepers or tax collectors. He hung around the wrong people, went to the wrong parties and chose the wrong trainees. He sided with the wrong crowd and took stands against those you were not supposed to oppose. And so whatever his view of Scripture was, we can be confident he did not hold it because others around him did or because it was taught in the synagogue school where he grew up.

The fact is that there were different views of Scripture in his own day. He had all the options open to him, and we have much evidence showing that he was willing to go with what was right, whether or not it was the view of his culture and peers. Given the other choices he made in his life, it would hardly make sense that on this issue he just conformed. With this in mind, let's consider several matters that reveal his view of the Scriptures.

## Divine Inspiration

First, Jesus speaks of God as the source of Scripture. As he addressed a testing (and probably a testy) question about marriage and divorce with the Pharisees, Matthew tells us that he said this:

> "Haven't you read," he replied, "that at the beginning the Creator 'made them male and female,' and said, 'For this reason a man will leave his father and mother and be united to his wife, and the two will become one flesh'?" (Matthew 19:4–5)

This is a reference to Genesis 2:24. In that passage it is the writer of Genesis who says, "For this reason a man will leave…" etc. But Jesus says, "The Creator made them and said, 'For this reason….'" These words were originally written down by the narrator of the book of Genesis (Moses), but Jesus credits the words to the Creator, to God himself. And so we can see that for Jesus to find something in Scripture was to find something that God said, something that had its origins with God. A later passage reinforces this:

> "But about the resurrection of the dead—have you not read what God said to you, 'I am the God of Abraham, the God of Isaac, and the God of Jacob'? He is not the God of the dead but of the living." (Matthew 22:31–32)

Jesus is quoting from Exodus 3:6. For him, something written in Scripture is the trustworthy word of God. A statement in John is even clearer:

> Jesus answered them, "Is it not written in your Law, 'I have said you are gods'? If he called them 'gods,' to whom the word of God came—and the Scripture cannot be broken—what about the one whom the Father set apart as his very own and sent into the world? Why then do you accuse me of blasphemy because I said, 'I am God's Son'?" (John 10:34–36)

Jesus equates the Law, the Scriptures and the word of God with one another. For Jesus to speak of one is to speak of the other. The quotation here is from the Psalms, a psalm not by David, but by Asaph, certainly a more obscure Biblical figure. But for Jesus this is not just the word of Asaph on a subject; it is the word of God. And so we can see that Jesus has the highest view of Scripture. For Jesus, when you have Scripture, you have word of God. The other things we will consider flow from this first point.

## 'And That's Final'

Second, what the Scripture taught settled an issue for Jesus. Some of you work in offices or plants where people have all different kinds of ideas about how something should be done. But when the big boss speaks (whoever he or she is), that settles it. For Jesus, Scripture had that power. If you were in a dispute over something and you could show what the Scriptures said—that settled it.

In Mark 12, Jesus tells the Parable of the Tenants. From the parallel passage in Luke 20, we can see that the people hearing it were struggling with the implications of the story, but Jesus settles it by saying, "Haven't you read this Scripture…" (Mark 12:10), and then he quotes Psalm 118:22–23. If they had doubts about what he was saying, he obviously felt that the Scripture could settle the matter and show that he was right.

Later in Mark 12, we see Jesus' belief that not knowing the Scriptures would lead to an inability to think something through clearly. To the Sadducees, who offered a complicated question about marriage after the resurrection, Jesus replied: "Are you not in error because you do not know the Scriptures or the power of God?…You are badly mistaken!" (Mark 12:24, 27) These Sadducees, who have been called the secular humanists of Jesus' day with their refusal to believe in an afterlife, thought they had a pretty airtight little riddle that would cause Jesus to stumble. But in so many words, he said to them, "You can't get this straight because you don't know the thing that gets people straightened out. You don't know the Scriptures."

For Jesus the Scriptures were the place to go to settle matters. The modern view of some religious leaders is that the Scriptures cannot be fully trusted because they are full of errors. Jesus, in quite the opposite view, believed that a mind would be filled with errors without the Scriptures. He saw the Scriptures as filled with truth—truth that would settle issues and resolve problems.

## Once and Future Truth

Third, Jesus had great confidence in the prophecies found in the Scriptures. For Jesus, Biblical prophecy was from God and had to be fulfilled. In the Gospels at least eleven times Jesus specifically called attention to how his life was fulfilling what had been written by the prophets. In addition there are twenty more times when the Gospel writers themselves pointed out how he was the fulfillment of Scripture.

It is clear that Jesus believed that Biblical prophecies were not just the speculations of men. They revealed the plans of God, and therefore, they had to be fulfilled. If Scripture promised something, then it would become a reality. No clearer statement of this can be found than in Jesus' comments to the disciples he met on the road to Emmaus:

> He said to them, "This is what I told you while I was still with you: Everything must be fulfilled that is written about me in the Law of Moses, the Prophets and the Psalms." (Luke 24:44)

The Scriptures "must be fulfilled." This one line tells us just about everything we need to know about the authority of the Scriptures. No one would ever say this about the words of men. (If I make a prediction, it may or may not come true.) But, to be like Jesus, we must acknowledge this about the promises of God. According to Jesus, in all that is happening, a plan is being worked out—a plan that was recorded accurately in the Scriptures and that the Scriptures say *must* happen.

## Scripture Soaked

Fourth, Jesus saturated his preaching and teaching with references to the Scriptures. Robert Coleman has identified ninety times in the Gospels when Jesus either quotes from the Scriptures, alludes to an event in Scripture or uses language similar to a Biblical expression.[1] If a modern reader finds himself or herself drawn to the books of Psalms and Isaiah in the Old Testament, such a person is in good company. Jesus quoted most often from these books, but he did use material from throughout the Scriptures.

When I contrast the physical ease with which I can access Scripture with the challenge it would have been for Jesus, I am all the more impressed. I can sit at my computer and do any number of sophisticated searches on my electronic Bible. I can click on a reference and instantly add it to my manuscript. I can even use my electronic palm device to search for a word or a verse while sitting in a restaurant. I do not know what all Jesus had to do just to read the Scriptures, but I do know that copies were not abundant and access to them was not easy. His little house in Nazareth almost certainly had no library. When we think of him running his busy carpenter's shop prior to his public ministry and how little time he would have had to study, we must marvel at the depth of his Biblical knowledge and how easily quotations flowed from his lips.[2]

While Jesus believed that he himself spoke the word of God, it is most important to observe how frequently he went to the Scriptures to support his message. It is also noteworthy that not once did he quote from the Apocrypha or other extra-Biblical and more recent (and supposedly relevant) books that were popular in his day. There was simply nothing for him that compared with the Scriptures and nothing that had the authority of the Scriptures. His example stated loud and clear that neither man's latest thinking nor long established traditions must be allowed to replace the word of God (Mark 7:13).

## Sword of the Spirit

Fifth, Jesus used the Scriptures frequently and personally in his own life. The Gospel writers do not provide an abundance of information about Jesus' personal meditations, but at two particularly difficult times in his life, we get a glimpse into how important the Scriptures were for him.

The first three Gospels all describe the time that he was tempted by Satan following his baptism. Significantly, with each temptation, Jesus responded with Scripture. Satan comes and says, "If you are the Son of God, tell these stones to become bread" (Matthew 4:3). Jesus responds with the words of Deuteronomy 8:3: "It is written: 'Man does not live on bread alone, but on every word that comes from the mouth of God'" (Matthew 4:4). Satan comes again and this time he quotes a Scripture back to Jesus and tempts him to jump from the top of the temple to allow God to save him. Jesus responds with Deuteronomy 6:16: "Do not put the Lord your God to the test" (Matthew 4:7). Finally, Satan offers him all the kingdoms of the world in exchange for just a moment of worship. Jesus says, "Away from me Satan," and returns once again to Deuteronomy, this time to 6:13, for these words: "For it is written: 'Worship the Lord your God, and serve him only'" (Matthew 4:10).

If this were all we knew about Jesus' relationship to the Scriptures, it would almost be enough. These were challenging moments. In times like these we need the most reliable help we can find. For Jesus there was nothing to compare with the Scriptures. When the pressure is on, where do you turn for strength, for guidance, for direction? When faced with big decisions and when dealing with crises in life, what do you set your mind on? Certainly, a theoretically high view of Scripture does not mean anything unless Scripture is where you go in these kinds of moments. Jesus' love for the Scriptures and his trust in them shines through in this most personal of times. Are we paying attention? Are we learning?

It is also in Jesus' last hours—even last moments—before his death that we see just how much the Scriptures meant to him. When the thought occurred that he might call down twelve legions of angels and save himself from the horror of the whole ordeal, he said, "But how then would the Scriptures be fulfilled that say it must happen in this way?" (Matthew 26:54). Isaiah 53 was most likely in his mind. To the very end he was focused on fulfilling what had been written. On the cross, becoming the ransom for many, Jesus contemplated his separation from God and with words of Psalm 22:1, cried "'Eloi, Eloi, lama sabachthani?'—which means, 'My God, my God, why have you forsaken me?'" (Mark 15:34). Moments later, he died with the words of Psalm 31:5 on his lips: "Into your hands I commit my spirit" (Luke 23:46). To the very end he had his mind and heart set on the Scriptures.

How did Jesus view the Scriptures? Did he see them as some people do, as just human literature? Certainly, he did not. Did he see them as significant writings, but writings that were sometimes in error? No, he saw them as the correction for error. Did he see them as important writings that needed to be supplemented by developing human traditions? Obviously, he did not. Human traditions and Scripture were not on the same ground. What is perfect needs no "human" improvements. Did he see the Scriptures as the authoritative word of God for our lives? Absolutely, he did.

If this was Jesus' view of the old covenant Scriptures, which all looked forward to his coming, it is clear that we should have an even higher view (if that is possible) of the new covenant Scriptures. They contain Jesus' very words and were written after his death and resurrection so that we might know him and his gospel. Of course, that which contains the fulfillment is even greater than that which foretold of his coming. Paul would later write: "All Scripture is God-breathed and is useful for teaching, rebuking, correcting and training in righteousness, so that the man of God may be thoroughly equipped for every good work" (2 Timothy 3:16–17). Is there any doubt that Jesus would have said "Amen"?

# 6
# The Kingdom of God

W hen you hear the word "anticipation" what comes to your mind? What I really mean to ask is what experience have you had with anticipation? Have there been times in your life when there was an expectation or a hope, and your body and mind just filled up with anticipation? Do you know the feeling I am describing? I would imagine that a recently engaged woman can understand what I am talking about. The relationship with her guy grew, as did her desire for greater closeness and for a commitment that would be long term. It all seemed to be going so well, but when would he pop the question? Why was he taking so long? Anticipation was something she and those close to her could almost measure—the waiting and the longing. She was fine once he asked, but the anticipation almost hurt.

Living in New England for fourteen years has given me a similar experience. I write this as spring training begins in preparation for another baseball season. There is one year that every Red Sox fan (and I am one) knows only too well: 1918. It has been eighty-four years since the home team won a World Series. In Boston, almost everyone can relate to anticipation. We can almost cut it with a knife, particularly on every evening that more than thirty thousand people jam into that little band box we call Fenway Park.

About one hundred and ninety years before Jesus began his ministry, a hero arose among the Jews and led his people to drive out the hated and barbarous Seleucids, some of the uncouth successors to Alexander the Great. Judas the Maccabee, and his equally zealous brothers, used stealth, cunning and courage to overcome far superior forces and give control of Israel back to the Jews. But by the time of Jesus, that sweet victory was like 1918 to a Red Sox fan, and once again the air was thick with anticipation. Sick of having their land occupied by foreigners who had no appreciation for their culture and no respect for their religion, the Jews longed for the Messiah who would deliver them. They looked for a Son of David who would once again lead Israel to be exalted among the nations. A then-popular poem from a work titled *The Psalms of Solomon* expressed what many Jews felt:

> Behold, O Lord, and raise up their king, the son of David,
>     at the time thou hast appointed, O God,
>     to reign over Israel thy servant.
> Gird him with strength to shatter wicked rulers.
> Cleanse Jerusalem from the Gentiles who trample and
>         destroy.
> In wisdom, in justice, may he thrust out sinners from
>         God's heritage,
>     crush the arrogance of the sinner like a potter's
>         crocks,
>     crush his whole substance with an iron mace,
>     blot out the lawless Gentiles with a word.
>     Put the Gentiles to flight with his threats.[1]

The Jews waited and hoped and longed for their savior, their redeemer, their Son of David. They lived in constant anticipation. They prayed for God to act, for him to break in, for him to vindicate them and show once more that Israel was the apple of his eye (Zechariah 2:8).

It was into this highly charged environment that Jesus came declaring, "The time has come. The kingdom of God is near. Repent and believe the good news!" (Mark 1:15). Virtually every word in that proclamation would have sent chills through the crowds. But what would come next was unexpected.[2] Almost all scholars, both those who have a loyalty to Jesus and those who write strictly as historians, are agreed on the fact that the center of Jesus' message is found in the words "the kingdom of God." Once Jesus comes with this announcement, says C. H. Dodd, "You no longer look for the reign of God through a telescope. No, you just open your eyes to see."[3] John Bright, in his classic study of the kingdom of God, notes that when we come to the New Testament, there is "a tremendous change of tense." The message of the Old Testament, he shows, is found in such statements as "Behold, the days are coming." The prophets speak in the future tense. But when Jesus arrives, it all changes: "The time has come."[4] The kingdom is coming now.

We have noted earlier that Jesus made some most amazing statements about his own identity, but it may surprise some to see that Jesus did not come primarily preaching himself. The focus of his message was not "look at me." His primary message was that the kingdom of God was breaking in and that men and women could be a part of it. The banquet table is prepared, and everyone is invited.

## But What Is the Kingdom?

As we have noted, Jesus' countrymen had some very definite ideas about the kingdom of God. In their minds it would be set up by a "Son of David," that is, one who would follow in David's footsteps in leading Israel to military and political victory. The kingdom would affirm again God's special relationship with the Jews and would put the Gentiles in their place—most likely in hell. Jesus grew up with all this. He would have heard such observations from all kinds of people coming in and going out of his carpentry shop. He would have known those who joined up with the nationalist group called the Zealots. It is likely that he had been encouraged to throw his lot in with them. But he was listening to another voice, and he was waiting for the right moment.

We cannot know all the ways Jesus' consciousness and understanding of his role were developed. However, from the things we have looked at in earlier chapters, we can be confident that he was doing just what we would expect, even with nationalist rhetoric all around him. He was listening to Scripture and he was having daily fellowship with his *Abba*, and all that eventually led him to the conviction that the time had come. He must have understood that the kingdom of God would be a fulfillment of Isaiah's vision, as opposed to a high-powered version of the Maccabean Revolt. It would be the peaceful kingdom where those from many nations beat their swords into plowshares (Isaiah 2:4). Here, old enemies would share life together (Isaiah 11). It would be established not by an aggressor, but by a servant (Isaiah 42:1). It would be a light to the Gentiles and all nations would flow to it (Isaiah 2:2, 9:1, 42:6, 49:6 and 51:4). This was quite a contrast with the popular revolutionary poetry. "The Son of David," says C. H. Dodd, "was supposed to cleanse Jerusalem *from* the Gentiles. Jesus wanted to cleanse it *for* the Gentiles."[5]

Jesus had to know that his message would get decidedly mixed reviews. He certainly had spent enough time pondering Isaiah 53 to know that some awful suffering lay ahead. So, surely, with a mixture of joy and dread, he put down his carpentry tools and stepped out to announce that the fulfillment of the ages was coming.

As much as Jesus talked about the kingdom, as many illustrations as he used for it, as many characteristics as he described of those who are in it, he never explicitly defined it. This tells me that we should be cautious about thinking we can quickly and precisely corral it. The more study I have done, the more I approach the whole concept with a sense of wonder, ever learning that it is more than I thought. I love going into the mountains. Give me a good mountain that I can drive around and look at from many different angles, and I will take that over the seashore any day (although that has its own dramatic beauty). I have come to think of the kingdom as a great mountain, which certainly fits with the imagery in Isaiah 2, and just when I think I know it well, I find something else amazing about it.

In doing research for this book, I would read one author and say, "That's it." Then I would read another and realize that the first author missed some things, but that he captured some other things that the second left out. And so it would go as I went from one book to the next. The idea of the kingdom seemed to be a moving target, but amazingly, I did not find this frustrating. The more I read (or the more I drove around the mountain), the more captivating it seemed to me. I could never feel that I had captured it, but I did feel privileged to contemplate it and be changed by it.

Jesus talked about the kingdom as something that was near, as something that had come upon us, as something within us, as something that was here, as something that would yet come. The scholars refer to the "now/not yet" paradox of the kingdom. That may be just the start of it. If you are one of those people who has to have everything in a nice, neat theological box, the idea of the kingdom is likely to drive you crazy. On the other hand, if you think you already have it in that box, I would encourage you to look again. It may be much more than you think. You may have moved on to your next project too quickly.[6]

"The kingdom of God" is a translation of the Greek phrase *basileia tou theou*. Most scholars believe a better rendering of *basileia* would be "reign" or "rule." This would lead to the conclusion that you have the kingdom when you have God in control, shaping and making us what we were meant to be. Now the Jews always believed God was ruling, but what they waited for was his rule to be manifested. In Jewish thought, reality was generally divided into two ages: the present age and the age to come. Jesus himself uses this terminology in Matthew 12:32 and Mark 10:30. The general belief was that when the kingdom of God came, the present age would end; and the people of God would be ushered into the age to come, where God's reign would be manifested completely. People lived in anticipation of "The Day of the Lord," believing that it would dramatically usher in the end of the present age and the beginning of the age to come.

With this background, Jesus announces something surprising. He preaches that the age to come (the reign of God) is breaking into the present age. We see this in statements like the one recorded by Luke: "But if I cast out demons by the

finger of God, then the kingdom of God has come upon you"
(Luke 11:20 NASB). The key phrase here is "come upon you."
The kingdom is breaking in. It is coming to a house near you.
The miracles that Jesus performed played a key role in
demonstrating that the kingdom was penetrating the present
age. John Bright describes it this way:

> To the New Testament faith the miracles which Jesus per-
> formed were not incidental or peripheral, but integral to
> his person. And they were understood eschatologically.
> That is, they were illustrations of the fact that in Christ the
> new age was even then intruding upon the present one: the
> power of the Kingdom of God was present in them and was
> grappling with the evil power of this age.[7]

Bright goes on to say that the miracles are mighty works
of the kingdom of God which are a taste of "the powers of the
age to come" which he finds reference to in Hebrews 6:5.
With the coming of the kingdom, the power of God is
released into our world of time and space. The kingdom is
like a tiny mustard seed that penetrates the soil, but will lead
to a large outcome (Matthew 13:31–32). The kingdom is like
yeast (or leaven) that can work its way into the whole lump
of dough (Matthew 13:33). The present age is not suddenly
coming to an end; but something totally new, with life-changing implications, is breaking into it.

Some of us would like to have a chart showing exactly
what the kingdom is, where it is, what it is like and exactly
who is in it. Jesus does not give us that. Instead, he paints a
variety of pictures for us. He says the kingdom is like a king
who prepared a wedding feast, like yeast, like a mustard seed,
like a net, like treasure in a field, like a man searching for fine
pearls, like a man who sows seed, like a king who wanted to

settle accounts or like a landowner who went to hire workers. And if we want to gain insight into the kingdom, we have to listen to each of Jesus' stories. We cannot capture the kingdom with just one of them, but each one helps us understand in a different way what it means that God is coming to us and that we are invited to accept his gifts.[8]

You may have found the kingdom, but the truth is, you will find the kingdom in new ways over and over again in your life. This transforms the whole idea of seeking the kingdom first (Matthew 6:33). Such a pursuit involves a lifetime. One may seek and find, but then discover that there is so much more to seek and to find. The kingdom for each of us is "now/not yet."

## What Does It Mean?

Before we go on, let's hold on to a few things: (1) the kingdom of God is coming in the life and the message of Jesus—the Spirit of the Lord is upon him, and he is bringing something that the world has never seen before; (2) this kingdom is not what the Jews were expecting—it turns out that the thoughts of men and the thoughts of God are just as different here as they have always been; and (3) the kingdom seems to mean a lot of different things, but the one thing that is clear is that when the kingdom comes to us, God is manifest in our lives.

Now to these we need to add two major ideas. *First, the announcement of the kingdom is good news*—and this is putting it mildly. It is the best news! It declares that God is coming for his people. As Jesus read in the synagogue in Nazareth, it is the time of God's favor. Something good, no, something wonderful, is headed our way. We are being given the invitation of a lifetime to come to the feast, to the banquet, to the celebration planned by God the Father (Matthew 22:2, Luke 13:29). In the United States we would feel pretty special if we were invited to a dinner at the White House. Nothing against the President, but this invitation from the Father and the Son makes that look pretty small in comparison.

What does this invitation really mean? Obviously, it is a metaphor for something; but what, exactly? This is such an important idea that it deserves more explanation, which we will get to in the next chapter. For now let us realize that accepting the invitation to the kingdom means having God with us to meet every need we have. For now, just hold on to the idea that we become recipients of God's undiscriminating generosity.

*The second idea is that life in the kingdom is so different that we can't possibly receive it without change.* The kingdom calls for a radical decision summed up in the word "repent." This may not have been the first word out of Jesus' mouth when he began his public ministry, but it is the first one recorded in the New Testament. The word in Greek is *metanoeo* (or in its noun form *metanoia*). When we hear "repent," most of us start thinking of the idea of being sorry for something or we think of some specific thing we need to stop or something we need to start. The word more literally means to turn the mind, as in a new direction. "The word certainly refers to spiritual turn around," writes Thomas Cahill, "but the change that is looked for here is an openness to something new and unheard of."[9] I would suggest that repentance has to do with developing a whole new attitude before it describes anything specific.[10] When the "age to come" breaks into this present age and you or I become a citizen of heaven, we enter a different world. We must be radically open to a whole new approach.

What will this new kingdom person look like? What will be the fundamental elements in his or her new attitude? The Gospels would seem to identify two of these.

First, there is humility. After apparently spending considerable time with Jesus, his disciples were still jockeying for position. "Who is the greatest in the kingdom?" they asked. Matthew describes Jesus' response:

> He called a little child and had him stand among them. And he said: "I tell you the truth, unless you change and become like little children, you will never enter the kingdom of heaven. Therefore, whoever humbles himself like this child is the greatest in the kingdom of heaven." (Matthew 18:2–4)

To these men who thought they had been "in" for a long time and were just trying to figure out how to elevate their rank, Jesus' words must have been sobering. They had not yet humbled themselves, and so they still stood outside the kingdom. They were with the right man, but their hearts still belonged to this present age. To give them a vivid picture of just how much change he was talking about, he picked up a toddler (*paidion*), and essentially said, "See this child? Unless you humble yourself like one of these, you will never enter the kingdom." We don't have to be smart to be in the kingdom. We don't have to perform at a certain level. We don't have to look a certain way. But we absolutely have to be humble. People who make light of their pride and manage to hold on to it are messing with something deadly. Humility is essential for kingdom living because God has so much to teach us. Besides, living in the kingdom is all about living daily in the presence of God, and no human being does this without humility.

Specifically, humility is demonstrated by becoming something that we saw earlier in chapter 3, which is at the essence of who Jesus was: a servant. As people enlist and follow the Servant-King, they too will become those with a mind-set to serve. On one occasion Jesus spoke of those who would put their hands to the plow and look back. He said they were not "fit for service in the kingdom of God" (Luke 9:62). The kingdom of God is a place where we serve. So no one is fit for the kingdom of God unless he or she desires to render service and to take the part of a servant.

Second, there is surrender. When we accept the reign of God, we give up our own personal reign. We will have a better context for this after the next chapter, but coming to the kingdom means trusting that God is God and that God is very good. It means letting go of our efforts to control and surrendering to God's will. In Matthew 6 we have some of Jesus' most familiar words:

> "Your kingdom come,
> your will be done
>     on earth as it is in heaven." (Matthew 6:10)

This verse is seen by scholars as an example of Hebrew parallelism (the best known quality in Hebrew literature) where the second line amplifies or explains the first. In this case, the kingdom comes when we have an attitude that wants God's will and not our own will. When you find kingdom people, you find those who submit and yield their wills to God's.

Whenever you have humility and surrender, you will have people who are in a state of *metanoia*. They are ready for baptism (Acts 2:38) and new birth (John 3:3–5). They will have much to learn, but the crucial fundamentals are in place. They will share in the kingdom. God is at work in their lives. The particulars will follow.

## But Isn't the Church the Kingdom?

For many believers it has been almost axiomatic that the kingdom of God and the church are the same thing.[11] What I am suggesting to those who have thought this is that we may have tried to push the kingdom into a box too small to hold it. As we have ˙observed, the kingdom is a magnificent concept, rich in meaning and application. Jesus most likely never tried to define it explicitly because it just refuses to be defined. Jesus surely perplexed those who wanted to be very precise about the kingdom when he spoke these words recorded by Luke:

> Once, having been asked by the Pharisees when the kingdom of God would come, Jesus replied, "The kingdom of God does not come with your careful observation, nor will people say, 'Here it is,' or 'There it is,' because the kingdom of God is within you." (Luke 17:20–21)

There you have it. The kingdom defies careful analysis and observation. Neither a scientist nor a logician can get his arms around it and say, "There! I got it! Here it is!" Yes, Jesus' words were probably addressed to those who would run to endorse the latest Messianic pretender, insisting, "This time I know that this is it." But there is something here about the inwardness of the kingdom that brings pause to anyone who thinks he knows its dimensions and precise location. Even saying, as some have, that the kingdom includes those whom God reigns over in heaven as well as those on earth still does not quite capture the spirit Jesus communicates here. You just cannot identify the kingdom with any one thing—even if it is a big thing. As Jesus' statement implies, the kingdom is a state of mind, a state of heart.

If you have what seems to be a careful study showing that the kingdom is the church, I am not suggesting that you throw it away. I am suggesting that you be open to a larger view. I believe you can hold on to the meat of what you have believed while allowing something quite exciting to be added to your plate. I believe that before we are done, we will see an even more dramatic relationship between the kingdom and the church.

In the first part of this chapter we looked at dozens of references to the kingdom in the Gospels that didn't mention the church. In truth, if we look at the fifty times the kingdom is mentioned in Matthew, the fifteen times it is mentioned in Mark and the thirty-eight times it is mentioned in Luke, we will only find one specific occasion when there is anything in the text that might cause us to directly connect the church with the kingdom. Of the remaining passages, there are a number that could fit with the understanding that the church and the kingdom are the same.

However, apart from the passage in Luke 17 that we have already looked at, I have identified several other texts for which this explanation does not seem to work at all. It is beyond the scope of this book to try to examine all of these or to do a detailed analysis of this subject, but I will take the time to look at two.

In Matthew 11, Jesus discusses the relationship of John the Baptist to the kingdom, and he says something quite enigmatic:

> "I tell you the truth: Among those born of women there has
> not risen anyone greater than John the Baptist; yet he who
> is least in the kingdom of heaven is greater than he. From
> the days of John the Baptist until now, the kingdom of

heaven has been forcefully advancing, and forceful men lay
hold of it." (Matthew 11:11–12)

I will leave it to greater minds than mine to exegete this text,
but I want us to notice just one thing. Whatever the kingdom
is, it had been forcefully advancing from the days of John the
Baptist until the time Jesus spoke these words, and not only
that, but forceful men were already laying hold of it. For obvious reasons, this does not fit with an understanding that the
kingdom and the church, which did not come until Pentecost
(Acts 2), are the same.

In Matthew 4:23 we find a passage the likes of which we
find several more times in the first three Gospels:

Jesus went throughout Galilee, teaching in their synagogues, preaching the good news of the kingdom, and
healing every disease and sickness among the people.

Three years before the church was established, Jesus was
preaching the good news of the kingdom in synagogues, on
hillsides and by the lake, and saying, "Repent and believe the
good news." He was preaching the kingdom to the crowds that
were harassed and helpless and in need of relief. He was telling
them that if they would seek first the kingdom and God's righteousness, everything else they needed would be given to them.
He was casting out demons and saying, "If I do this by the
finger of God, then the kingdom of God is come upon you."
He was watching a rich man walk away from his offer and
saying, "How hard it is for the rich to enter the kingdom of
God." If we try to hold fast to a thesis that the kingdom did not
come until the church began on Pentecost, there is something
about all this that just doesn't make sense. If anything is clear
in Jesus' message, it is that he believed that the time had come,

God was at work, the kingdom was breaking in and men could lay hold of it.

So what do we do with a passage like Mark 9:1? There Jesus says, "I tell you the truth, some who are standing here will not taste death before they see the kingdom of God come with power." In our normal reading of it, this seems to support the idea that the kingdom had not yet come, which sounds like a good fit with the events recorded later in Acts 2. But if the kingdom did not come until Pentecost, how do we reconcile this with what we have just looked at?

Perhaps these various passages provide more evidence for the idea that we just cannot put the kingdom in a neat box. However, I would suggest that there may be a better explanation. The various texts indicate that the kingdom comes in waves. John says it is near and to get ready. Jesus calls people to believe the good news about it. He tells people to seek it above all else. He says it has come upon his hearers. He says forceful men are entering it. It is breaking in. It starts out as a mustard seed, but it gains momentum. But while the kingdom was coming, we now know that it would not come in its full power until the Son of God laid down his life as a ransom and until he burst out of the tomb on the third day. Until that happened, the whole enterprise was in question. In this context, Jesus could not have been saying that the kingdom had not come at all. Instead he was saying that it would not come with "Category 5"-force until later. Its meaning and legitimacy would not really be established until it had conquered death. He claimed that some standing there would live to see it (and most of them did).[12]

What then is the relationship between the kingdom and the church? While there are any number of reasons to say that the kingdom and the church are not the same, there is good reason to say that the two are about as closely related as two things can be. Jesus clearly believed he was bringing something brand new. The old wineskins would not hold the new wine. Judaism could not be reformed. God did not intend for it to be. There would be a new Israel which would include, in fulfillment of Isaiah, men and women from all nations. As the kingdom broke in, it would need to be embodied in a community. Isaiah's prophecies indicated it would be a place where people treated each other in new ways.

Clearly understanding this, Jesus never intended to just throw his message out there and see what happened. He came to call together a people who would then work together to herald the message. He started with the Twelve, eventually saw the group grow to seventy-two, and after his resurrection, the number was up to 120. At a crucial point in his relationship with the Twelve, Matthew records this exchange, giving an understanding of his plan:

> "But what about you?" he asked. "Who do you say I am?" Simon Peter answered, "You are the Christ, the Son of the living God."
>
> Jesus replied, "Blessed are you, Simon son of Jonah, for this was not revealed to you by man, but by my Father in heaven. And I tell you that you are Peter, and on this rock I will build my church, and the gates of Hades will not overcome it. I will give you the keys of the kingdom of heaven; whatever you bind on earth will be bound in heaven, and whatever you loose on earth will be loosed in heaven." Then he warned his disciples not to tell anyone that he was the Christ. (Matthew 16:15–20)

This is the only place in the Gospels where we find the words "kingdom" and "church" being discussed in the same context. Jesus does not equate the church and the kingdom, but he links the ideas together. He is going to build his church—his *ecclesia,* his community, the new people of God—on the truth that he is the Son of God. In connection with this, he tells Peter he will give him the keys to the kingdom. The church, here represented by Peter, will be the instrument of God in the world used to make the kingdom known. Once the church is established, the same response that brings one into the kingdom brings him into the community and the fellowship. I would suggest this means that the church is the group of people on earth who have accepted the good news of the kingdom, the people who have submitted themselves to the reign of God. Is the church the kingdom? Not really. Are all those in the church in the kingdom? Absolutely. Today when we proclaim the good news of the kingdom, must we always call men and women to commit to the common life in the church? Without a doubt. It is only in the fellowship of the church that any of us will get the help and encouragement we need to keep seeking first the kingdom. It is only in our unity with others in the church that we have any hope of being the shining city on a hill that Jesus said kingdom people would be.[13]

Here is the conclusion to the matter: The God of the universe has invaded our planet. He came in Jesus of Nazareth. The age to come has already broken into the present age. As we will see in the next chapter, this means that reality is on our side. Now that this has been made plain, there is nothing more important than seeking the kingdom of God. We must make the kingdom, the reign of God, our greatest passion. It is like a great treasure found in a field, worth the sacrifice of all we have (Matthew 13:44). It is like the pearl of great price that a man would sell everything to gain (Matthew 13:45–46). Living with the values of the kingdom brings us into powerful relationships in the church, with others who are kingdom-minded. The kingdom will forever be a community of those with changed lives who are now ready to live as servants.

The coming of the kingdom in all that Jesus was, all that he taught and all that he did, represents the most crucial event in human history, for it was there that our history was intersected by the divine. We can keep living as if there is only this present age, or we can open our eyes and see that light has broken into the darkness.

And here is the remarkable thing: the kingdom of God comes with power—miracle power, resurrection power, life-changing power—but it does not come like storm troopers, requiring our obedience with the use of force. It comes like an invitation to a feast issued by a gentle servant who does not break bruised reeds or snuff out smoldering wicks (Isaiah 42:1–3). He will live for us. He will serve us. He will die for us. But he will not force us into his kingdom. All who are there, are there because they have been impressed with an incomprehensible display of love and have accepted a gracious invitation.

In the kingdom of God, an amazing new order of life is offered to us. What choice are *you* making?

# 7
# His Good News:
## Extravagant Generosity

D o you enjoy a party? Do you welcome a chance to celebrate? I wrote earlier about the angst suffered by those of us who are Boston Red Sox fans. The rest of the story is that in 2002 New Englanders celebrated what has probably become the biggest sports prize of all. Our football Patriots shocked the world—and some of us—by winning the Super Bowl against the high-octane St. Louis Rams. You could hear the shouting all over the region. I am not sure we still can believe it, but I do know that the celebrating went on for days. About 1.2 million happy souls poured into downtown Boston with the wind chill factor hovering near zero to do one thing: celebrate.

When Jesus of Nazareth announced that the kingdom of God he was ushering in was like a feast or like a banquet, people should have known that this was not your run-of-the-mill apocalyptic prophet. The declaration should have given his listeners a clue that there was something unusually upbeat about this man's message. Sure, Jesus would talk of judgment and the consequences of sin and self-centeredness, because that was a part of reality; but his overriding message was that God is good and that he is out to do good to you and me, as well as to people we would not even think he would like.

Scholars and commentators have chosen a number of different phrases to sum up what Jesus preached. Andrew Greely talks about "the insanely generous love of God," arguing that the novel element in Jesus' good news is that God's love is so powerful that it pushes him to the point of insanity.[1] This is a word we will come back to later. C. H. Dodd finds in Jesus' preaching "the undiscriminating generosity of the heavenly Father."[2] Both of these scholars are hitting on something that was brought home to me several years ago. At one point in the Sermon on the Mount, Jesus said:

> "Which of you, if his son asks for bread, will give him a stone? Or if he asks for a fish, will give him a snake? If you, then, though you are evil, know how to give good gifts to your children, how much more will your Father in heaven give good gifts to those who ask him!" (Matthew 7:9–11)

Someone, now forgotten, I am sorry to say, helped me focus on the idea of "the much more of the heavenly Father." To this day I often think of that phrase when wondering how something will turn out. The idea is the same as that found by the scholars. Jesus is telling us that what God wants to do for us in his kingdom is incredibly more than we can ask or imagine. We have our ideas about what it means to be generous, but God does "much more." Putting all this together, it seems appropriate for us to speak of the extravagant generosity of God.

Every standard Jesus sets for us, every challenge he gives us, every seemingly impossible moral imperative he announces must be seen in the context of this insanely generous love, this abundance of support, this extravagant generosity. Take away this gift, this offer, this lavishing of grace, and the call to follow Jesus would just be too hard, the Sermon on the Mount would be a burden, and the idea of seeking first the will of God would wear us down. However, words like "joy," "glad" and "gladness" show up often in the Gospels.

These documents describe some tough things that we will face, but they are not gloomy works. This is all because of "the much more of the heavenly Father." The life of a disciple of Jesus, which we will examine later, can be challenging, stressful and even exhausting at times; but it is overshadowed and undergirded by a God who gives lavishly and supplies all that is needed—and much more.

Those who follow Jesus are called to help others find the kingdom, but it is important for us to realize that we are not called just to guide others through a series of Bible studies (although this is usually needed). We are called first and foremost to announce a banquet and invite people to a feast. We are called to do as Jesus did and declare the amazing generosity of God, the abundance of grace and a love that almost borders on the insane. Whenever people spend time with disciples of Jesus, they should notice this coming from our hearts, even in the hard times.

## A Parable and An Event

I believe what I have said about the extravagance of God's generosity to be absolutely true, but let us go to the Gospels and hear Jesus describe this in his various and memorable ways.

No parable of Jesus captures the abundant way God loves us—especially when we have made a total mess of things—as does the story of the lost son. Luke 15 starts with the story of a shepherd who leaves his ninety-nine sheep to go look for one that is lost. It continues with the story of a homemaker who loses one of her ten coins and then spares nothing in her effort to find it. The first point in both parables seems to be the extraordinary effort (and the risky one, in the case of the shepherd) that was made to find what was lost. The second point in both cases is that there was an "over the top" celebration when what was lost was found. It is good to have your sheep back, but does that really call for getting in touch with all the friends and neighbors? And we can all relate to finding some lost money, but would we ordinarily invite the neighborhood to come over for a party after finding it? So what is Jesus' message? "God's passion for his people is so great," observes Andrew Greely, "that he dispenses with the normal canons of discretion and good taste in dealing with us."[3] As strong as the message is in these two stories, as much as they say about how God is willing to love us absurdly, they are just the warm-up acts.

The main story in the chapter describes an ungrateful son, who asked for his share of the inheritance. Thinking only of himself, he headed out on his own adventure. Soon he had blown everything his father gave him, on wild and crazy living. His situation got worse when his adopted country found itself in drought and famine. Desperate for anything, he hired on with, apparently, a non-Jewish fellow who put him to work on his pig farm. We are not told how it all worked, but it seems the pigs ended up eating better than he did. Finally, he had a right thought: "Those guys who work for my Father for minimum wage are doing better than I am. I will go back and apologize and hope my father will at least let me be one of his hired men."

Perhaps still rehearsing his confession and far enough away to be only a distant figure to anyone at the homestead, he suddenly saw a shocking sight. It was his father running toward him on the road. The man had no weapon. He actually looked happy. Within moments the prodigal found himself, embarrassingly, being hugged and kissed by a grown man. He stammered out his prepared speech about not deserving anything, but his father was paying no attention to him. Instead he was busy ordering the servants to bring a robe, sandals and a ring. He was orchestrating a feast and a celebration. Observes Greely, "Only a slightly demented father would shower honor on him who was a wastrel."[4]

Unlike in the first two stories (Luke 15:7 and 10), Jesus does not give us the spiritual application this time. Apparently, the point is plenty clear. Yes, it is clear, but it is unbelievable. We have a God who is like that. He doesn't act cool. He doesn't play it close to the vest. He doesn't conceal his emotions. He just loves us extravagantly, even when we are a mess. This is the good news of the kingdom—a bit on the dangerous side!

If that was true of a parable, it was even more true of something that happened in real life. John has a story in his Gospel about a woman caught in the very act of adultery. The story is in John 8 and most translations indicate that it is not found in some of the oldest manuscripts, but there is broad agreement about its authenticity.

The account finds Jesus in Jerusalem at one of those times only mentioned by John. It appears that it was about six months before Jesus would come back there for the Passover and the final events of his life. After a night camped out on the Mount of Olives, Jesus rose early and made his way to the temple courts where he found an opportunity to teach and discuss the good news of the kingdom. A rude interruption by the Pharisees and teachers of the law gave him the opportunity to illustrate what it was all about.

The local "morals police" had apparently been keeping watch on people's lives, or perhaps, more odiously, setting a trap for a victim. At any rate, these religious teachers come into Jesus' meeting with a woman whom they say was caught in adultery. Since the man involved is nowhere to be seen, we might suspect that he escaped. Perhaps he was just a part of the trap that had been set, since the entire situation was being orchestrated to discredit Jesus. Obviously, these teachers knew that they didn't need an opinion from an itinerant preacher from Galilee. The day before, they had made enough fun of where he was from (John 7:52). With their motives obviously transparent, the Pharisees pressed on to ask how Jesus would rule in this case.

They reminded him that the Law of Moses required stoning, and they wanted to know what he would say. There was something of a bluff here, since the Jews could no longer carry out capital punishment. Only the Roman procurator could enforce that, and he was not likely to approve something of this nature.

What Jesus did next is enigmatic. He stooped down and began writing on the ground with his finger. We have no idea what he wrote; but whatever he wrote, it did not stop the challenges. What he said next, however, did have impact. "If any one of you is without sin, let him be the first to throw a stone at her" (John 8:7). After more writing on the ground, he looked up to see the crowd of accusers drifting away until the last was gone. With no one left to charge her, the legal case was over. John ends the account with these words:

> Jesus straightened up and asked her, "Woman, where are they? Has no one condemned you?"
> "No one, sir," she said.

"Then neither do I condemn you," Jesus declared. "Go
now and leave your life of sin." (John 8:10–11)

God's extravagant generosity did not just make a good
story like the one in Luke 15. Jesus did not just preach it. He
put it into practice in real life. Jesus did not ignore the fact that
the woman had her own culpability, but he showed her that
there was at least one man and the one God who could offer
her forgiveness and a fresh start. She may have been a prostitute. John does not say, but from the references in Matthew 21
and the story in Luke 7, we know that some with that background were coming to Jesus and to the kingdom. Whatever
her story, she had to have left this experience understanding
that God is amazingly generous and full of grace. The religious
police did not condemn her that day—they just wandered off.
Jesus, on the other hand, looked her in the face and clearly
communicated, "I don't condemn you." I doubt she ever forgot those words. No condemnation!

We don't know what happened to her, but we can imagine
some things that could have very easily taken place. We can
imagine that six months later she heard about his trial and his
crucifixion. Perhaps she heard the noisy crowd and looked out
to see a man she remembered well, as he struggled under the
weight of a huge beam, on his way to the city garbage dump
for crucifixion. Perhaps fifty days later she was in the crowd
during Pentecost and heard Peter preaching about the one
who showed mercy. There were likely many in that group who
could remember their personal encounters with him. Perhaps
she was one of the three thousand who said, "Yes, I want to follow him." It could have happened just that way because grace
has just that kind of impact.

## Responding Radically

We could go on at length here. These stories are not atypical. The parable of the man forgiven the huge debt, the justification of the tax collector who prayed with the Pharisee, the story of Zacchaeus, the forgiveness of the woman at Simon's house, the parable of the workers in the vineyard, the support for the man who confessed his doubt, the numerous healings of those with demon possession, the cleansing of the ten lepers (nine of whom were less than grateful), the forgiveness of the thief on the cross—all of these speak of God's extravagant generosity. In addition, we have the fact that the core group of the new people of God had failed at the crucial hour and were therefore in their roles only because of the relentless grace of their leader. Surely, this was something the early church never forgot.

Matthew records two short parables to show the greatness of the kingdom.

> "The kingdom of heaven is like treasure hidden in a field. When a man found it, he hid it again, and then in his joy went and sold all he had and bought that field.
> "Again, the kingdom of heaven is like a merchant looking for fine pearls. When he found one of great value, he went away and sold everything he had and bought it."
> (Matthew 13:44–46)

Nothing can compare with the kingdom of God because in it we find this inexhaustible generosity and abundance. But these two parables also show that there is something so great in the kingdom that the only appropriate response is a radical one. Whatever we give up to have the kingdom, we can easily afford to give up, because in the kingdom we find "the *much more* of the heavenly Father."

In the kingdom of God we will be treated by the Father in gracious ways we cannot possibly deserve. But we must not misunderstand. The good news is not that we can just stay the way we are and be accepted by God. The good news is that in the kingdom we find enough abundance to help even people like us to change in major ways. Getting help like this is worth any sacrifice. It does, in fact, require a sacrifice of all, but what would we expect to give for something of such inestimable value? The men in the parables had no qualms about giving all. They realized the value of what they had found.

His critics were more right than they realized. Jesus was "the friend of sinners" (Luke 7:34). In Jesus all of us are loved unconditionally, unreservedly, embarrassingly, amazingly. God wants us to call him *Abba,* and he is not the least bit reserved about being that for us. How would it change you if in the core of your being, you were filled with a conviction about "the much more of the heavenly Father" and the extravagant generosity of God? As Jesus said, "Repent and believe the good news!" We simply need to change our minds and accept the fact that God really is this good.

# Kingdom Attitudes

In the minds of many people, religion is primarily about the regulation of behavior. As such, much of religion has been a dull and dreary thing. On the other hand, the kingdom of God as Jesus preached it was about the transformation of people's hearts and the creation of new attitudes. Jesus was concerned about behavior. But that's not where he started. He taught that truly righteous behavior flows from within and that no enforcement of behavior will bring people life if they do not become new on the *inside*. There is probably no better summary of the new attitudes that will characterize people of the kingdom than those found at the beginning of the Sermon on the Mount, in what we usually call the "Beatitudes."

Moses went up on the mountain and came down with the Ten Commandments. Matthew in his Gospel shows Jesus to be the new and greater Moses. Like the Old Testament giant, Jesus is on a mountain, but he gives no commandments engraved on stone tablets. Instead, he gives eight attitudes that are to be enshrined in our hearts (Matthew 5:1–12). These attitudes are both a response to the generosity of God and the qualities that lead to experiencing his gifts in ongoing and in greater ways.

If we have ever thought much about the Beatitudes, we usually have focused on some of the more difficult things they seem to require of us. It may be helpful to continue the theme of the previous chapter of this book by noticing first what they promise to bring:

- The kingdom of heaven
- Comfort
- Inheriting the earth
- Being filled
- Mercy
- Seeing God
- Being called sons of God
- A great reward in heaven

It is not uncommon for people to begin to question what Jesus meant by "poor in spirit" or "meekness" and not see that Jesus is, in essence, saying, "Here are the attitudes my Father wants to bless, and here are the attitudes that he does bless." In other words, he is saying, "Here are the attitudes that cause our generous God to give and support and enrich us even more." Maybe a more correct way of saying it is, "Here are attitudes that free us up so we can receive even more of God's blessings and generosity." Whatever else the Beatitudes are, they are the key to the storehouse of God's abundance. The more they become who we are, the more we experience the overflow of God's love and commitment to us.

I recently purchased one of the popular handheld devices that are really minicomputers. I was especially happy to get it because there was software available that enables one to load the entire Bible onto the device. After downloading the software to the "PDA" from my laptop computer, nothing was happening. The file management screen showed that the text had been installed, but I could not access it. A computer-savvy friend took a quick look at it and said, "Oh, it looks like you don't have the reader." So, the entire Bible was there, but I could not receive its blessings because in my haste, I had not installed a small file that would enable me to read all the data.

In many ways the Beatitudes are like that reader. They are attitudes that enable us to see clearly what God is doing, and they open even greater doors that allow the blessings of God to flow. His generosity and his abundance are always there, but we need the right attitudes of heart to "read" them and gain full access to them.

I once regarded the Beatitudes as an italicized poem to kick off the Sermon on the Mount, and because I have never been a big fan of poetry, I would skip through it hurriedly in an effort to get to something more practical. And then one day it occurred to me that the Master Teacher put these eight statements at the beginning of his message for a very good reason. I looked back at Matthew 4 and saw that Jesus came to call people to repent, that is, to turn their minds in a new direction. Then it occurred to me that the Sermon on the Mount, which pretty much follows that statement, is really a description of how our minds will work when they are turned toward God. The Beatitudes describe the basic and fundamental change that will lead to the blessings described in the sermon. I could not have been more wrong in skipping through them to get to the "good stuff." The Beatitudes are the key kingdom attitudes. We must be in the process of developing them to even enter the kingdom, and we must be growing in them to mature in the kingdom. There is little or nothing in the rest of the New

Testament that pertains to life and lifestyle that is not rooted in these kingdom attitudes.

As we prepare to look at these statements, I must caution you that they offer a message that has not been embraced by many in our generation. A best-seller a few years back was titled *All I Really Need to Know I Learned in Kindergarten*. I am sure the book had some cute advice, but I don't think any of us were taught the message of the Beatitudes in kinder-garten—or in any other school situation—and most of all, we did not get it from television or other voices of pop culture. Very few of us learned these from Mom or Dad's example. Actually, the lessons in the Beatitudes pretty much turn our world upside down. If the Beatitudes have appeared to you as benign platitudes, you are not hearing them. They call for a radical, some would say foolish, change of direction. Upon close examination, they seem almost to be from another plan-et, and that is not far from the truth. They are the attitudes of those who are taking their direction from heaven.

## Poor in Spirit

Jesus begins by saying, "Blessed are the poor in spirit, for theirs is the kingdom of heaven" (Matthew 5:3). Right at the beginning, he throws us a curve ball. We would almost have expected Jesus to say, "Blessed are the rich in spirit." After all, isn't it better to be rich in spirit than to be rich in material things? Don't we want to have an abundance of spiritual qual-ities? What does Jesus have in mind?

In the Greek language there were two common words for "poor." One word meant poor to the point that one did not own property. The other, *ptochos,* the one found here, was used to describe a beggar, or one in desperate circumstances.

It sounds as if Jesus is saying the person who will be blessed is the person who realizes and acknowledges that he is a spiritual beggar. This, in fact, fits very well with other teachings that we hear from Jesus. In one of his more famous parables, he tells of the Pharisee and the tax collector who both went up to the temple to pray (Luke 18:9–14). The Pharisee prayed about himself (several translations say "to himself"). He was confident in his own righteousness and believed his behavior made him right before God. As he saw himself, he was "rich in spirit," and his self-confidence bubbled over. The other man was a disreputable tax collector, who apparently was very much in touch with his own failures and sins. He knew he could not come to God and boast of his deeds. All he could do was confess his spiritual bankruptcy and throw himself on the mercy of God ("God, have mercy on me, a sinner"). In what would have been a shocking conclusion to the story for those in the Jewish establishment, Jesus has the tax collector going home justified before God, and the other man lost and outside the kingdom.

The Sermon on the Mount has sometimes been seen as an ethic that is impossible to live and a standard that imposes an enormous burden on those who try to live it. Such thinking almost always fails to realize that the sermon starts with this beatitude—which is a ringing declaration of our need for God's grace. Men and women must be willing to face their sin and failures and admit their desperate need for God. God promises to bless this attitude with such a truckload of grace that the humble soul is brought right into the kingdom and given all the rights and privileges of citizenship.[1]

In a culture in which we are told to think highly of ourselves, focus on our assets, and never feel bad about ourselves,
Jesus' message is not always welcomed. His terminology may
be familiar enough to be "acceptable" (or ignored), but once
people begin to know what it means, they usually take great
exception to it. Not many of us are happy to embrace the fact
that we have sinned and that our sin has put us in deficit.

Spiritual truth in general and Jesus' teachings in particu-
lar are filled with ironies and paradoxes. It is in seeing how
serious our sin is and how utterly helpless we are to remedy
the situation that we are freed up to receive the blessings of
the kingdom and become more than we could have ever
dreamed. At the core of the idea of being poor in spirit is an
attitude of humility which squares with reality, connects us to
God, and puts us on a track to live life to the full.

It was was D. M. Lloyd-Jones's book, *Studies in the Sermon
on the Mount,*[2] which I read more than twenty years ago, that
first helped me see that the Beatitudes should probably be
thought of as a progression and not as a group of eight dis-
connected ideas that could be rearranged in any order. The
more I examined this premise, the more true it seemed to be.
The first beatitude is the key to the others and the second one
follows logically, and so it goes throughout the eight statements. If this is as true as I believe it to be, then there is no
way to jump to being pure in heart or being a peacemaker.
There are other changes to make first.

But we must be careful here. Becoming poor in spirit is
not somehow the first block that you step on, on your way to
bigger and better things. Becoming poor in spirit is an attitude
that must be there at the beginning and remain with us all the
way through.[3] We must allow life and circumstances and our

own actions and attitudes to bring us back to this beatitude again and again. I have been a part of many efforts in the last thirty years to build churches that would please God. Every effort succeeded in some ways, but each effort also caused us to see our sin and made clear our poverty of spirit. For this I am thankful. Whenever we lose this attitude or turn away from it, we lose the gospel and its power. The Sermon on the Mount, with its unbelievably high calling, has a way of humbling us and bringing us back to this beatitude and our need for God again and again. This is not a bad thing, for those who are poor in spirit keep finding the kingdom.

## Those Who Mourn

I have found many interpretations of the Beatitudes to be less than satisfying, and I especially begin to feel this whenever I come to the second of these. "Blessed are those who mourn," Jesus said, "for they will be comforted" (Matthew 5:4). In the first place, many commentaries make nothing of the connection between this beatitude and the first one. Even some of my favorite authors make this mistake.[4] In the second place, many seem to take this verse out of the basic context of Jesus' teaching. Many writers begin to talk here about mourning over the condition of the world. Others see this as Jesus declaring a blessing on all who suffer. At least one writer I respect thinks that this refers to refusing to accommodate ourselves to the world's standard. By ignoring the connection with the first beatitude, these writers miss the fact that the basic message of the gospel is seen in these two beatitudes and in the way the second follows the first.

"Blessed are those who mourn." Having faced our sin, our failures and our spiritual bankruptcy, we now calculate the impact of our sinful hearts and sinful behavior. We experience what Paul will later call "godly sorrow" (2 Corinthians 7:10–11). We mourn over what we have become and what we have done to God and to others. We take ownership of our sin. We feel grief because of those we have hurt. The prophet Jeremiah condemned those in his day who dared to "dress the wound of my people as though it were not serious. 'Peace, peace,' they say, when there is no peace" (Jeremiah 8:11). The person who mourns over his sin says, "My sin is serious and I must not treat it lightly."

The talk show divas will tell us to be nice to ourselves. The latest best-seller will tell us not to focus on negative things. But Jesus teaches us that the way to real healing and change is to mourn over what we have done and the hurt that it caused. When we are fully in touch with the sin we have committed—and more than that, the sinners that we are— then we are ready to receive the blessing Jesus promises: we will be comforted. God's grace will embrace us. We will not be left in despair. We will be raised up. Isaiah's prophecy that Jesus read in the synagogue in Nazareth will be fulfilled in us. On those who grieve, God will bestow a "crown of beauty instead of ashes, the oil of gladness instead of mourning, and a garment of praise instead of a spirit of despair" (Isaiah 61:3).

Jesus' message is entirely consistent with the message we find in the book of Psalms. After sinning grievously, David finally grasped the horrible effects of his heart and behavior. He mourned over his sin. Then after experiencing God's mercy, he wrote:

> The sacrifices of God are a broken spirit;
>    a broken and contrite heart,
> O God, you will not despise. (Psalm 51:17)

Those who are poor in spirit and those who mourn over their sin are welcomed into the kingdom where God's grace is lavished on them. The very thing the world tells us to avoid is the thing that brings us God's refreshment.

## The Meek

When we come to the third beatitude, we surely come to the one that has been the most ridiculed.[5] "Blessed are the meek," said Jesus, "for they will inherit the earth" (Matthew 5:5). I think immediately of a T-shirt message that I have seen many times: "If the meek inherit the earth, what is going to happen to us tigers?" About the last thing in the world people want to be is meek. There are two problems here. The first is that we often don't understand what this word means. The second is that even when we do understand it, it does not describe anything we instinctively want to be.

The word in Greek is *praus*. William Barclay tells us that this word was used to describe a wild animal that had learned to accept control.[6] In that vein it was used to describe a powerful stallion after it was broken. The idea is that those who have this quality become gentle, humble and most of all, teachable. Can we see the connection with the first two beatitudes? We have faced our sin and we have taken seriously the consequences. But we have also received God's grace and comfort that we know we do not deserve. If this has happened, we are now in a humble state, realizing how much we need to listen and learn. A defensive spirit is gone, and we are ready to be trained in this new way of life that we have found in the kingdom. This third beatitude is absolutely critical for living as a disciple of Jesus. I have observed how, over time, we can lose this attitude and heart when we do not return often to the first two beatitudes, remembering that we have been cleansed of our past sins (2 Peter 1:9). The loss of this attitude of meekness and humility is spiritually devastating. I find some older disciples far too cavalier about this. We do not love someone when we see them wandering from a meek and humble heart and give no warnings.

Those who are meek, humble and teachable "will inherit the earth." Each of these beatitudes describes the way God will bless those in his kingdom. This is one of many places where it is evident to me that Jesus was not just teaching us something that would "get us to heaven" but was showing us how to live life to the full on Earth. Those who are clothed with humility will learn the most and make the most of their lives in this world. Sure, heaven awaits them—but the blessings of humility pay dividends even now.

## Those Who Hunger and Thirst

I have learned that God's truth is not always something that fits nicely with human judgment, but in this case, the fourth beatitude follows the first three in a very logical fashion. "Blessed are those who hunger and thirst for righteousness," Jesus says, "for they will be filled" (Matthew 5:6). If we have seen our spiritual bankruptcy or emptiness, honestly faced the pain caused by our sin, recognized our need to be learners, and grasped the depths of God's love for us, the next step is clearly to pursue what comes from God that can fill us up. To hunger and thirst for righteousness is quite at odds with the normal hungers of the human heart, but having seen our need for God and the failure of our own devices, we now know what really matters.

The man or woman in the kingdom longs to find God's will and do it. Righteousness in the Scriptures is much more than religious perfection or the observance of rules of morality. It is faithfulness in relationships.[7] Those who hunger for this will be filled—filled with richness in relationships. Nothing matters more. This is what life is about and it doesn't get any better than this![8]

## The Merciful

It has been suggested that the first four beatitudes have to do with restoring our relationship with God and being enriched in that relationship. The person who has plunged into the first four beatitudes has experienced the generosity of God that we looked at in chapter 7. He has seen his need and felt God's grace. He has been treated with mercy. He knows that he is the ten million dollar debtor who has been forgiven (Matthew 18:23–27). He is now being graciously trained and shown a new way of life. The last four beatitudes, it seems, have to do with how the kingdom person interacts with others. He hungers to be filled with righteousness, and righteousness has everything to do with his relationships.

We next hear Jesus say, "Blessed are the merciful, for they will be shown mercy" (Matthew 5:7). What is the first thing we should expect of someone who has been treated with abundant mercy? We expect him to show mercy to others. The shocking part about the story of the forgiven debtor is that in Jesus' parable, he experienced such vast forgiveness, yet was extremely unmerciful to another person who owed him a much smaller amount (Matthew 18:28–30). If we have been shown mercy, we must in turn show it to others.

The follower of Jesus understands that imitating the mercy of God does not just mean a willingness to forgive. It means a willingness to sacrifice ourselves in order to bring forgiveness, help and comfort to others. If this is not yet clear, we will certainly see it when we look at the cross in chapter 11. This is where God's wisdom begins to look quite foolish to the world. But Jesus promises that those who show mercy (because they have already received so much from God) will be shown even more mercy. The old adage that you cannot out-give God will be proven true.[9]

## The Pure in Heart

The importance of a pure heart is certainly a consistent theme throughout the Scriptures. David, in the aforementioned Psalm 51, cried out, "Create in me a pure heart, O God" (Psalm 51:10). Isaiah proclaimed God's judgment on those who honored God with their lips while their hearts were in a far different place (Isaiah 29:13). Purity of heart is about genuineness and sincerity. It is about letting the inside be cleansed so that the outside will then take care of itself (Matthew 23:26). In the sixth beatitude Jesus says, "Blessed are the pure in heart, for they will see God" (Matthew 5:8).

Had I arranged the Beatitudes, I would have probably thought this statement should come first. After all, what is more important than a pure heart? Proverbs tell us, "Above all else, guard your heart, for it is the wellspring of life" (Proverbs 4:23). While this is true, there is probably a good reason that this beatitude comes later and not first. Biblically, the way to arrive at purity of heart is to come to God, admitting how impure our hearts are. David wrote, "The sacrifices of God are a broken spirit; a broken and contrite heart, O God, you will not despise" (Psalm 51:17). The idea is that, as we come to God with hearts contrite over our sin, the work of grace can begin in us and bring us to a place we could not reach on our own. David's earlier request for God to create in him a pure heart, is a reminder that we cannot clean up our own hearts, but we get to this point only after becoming humble before God. Brokenness and humility before God is what the first four beatitudes are all about. Only God can bring us to purity of heart.

Given my thinking about the progression of the Beatitudes, you may ask why this one is not the fifth rather than the sixth. Why would it not come after hungering and thirsting for righteousness? Wouldn't purity of heart be the attitude that leads to showing mercy? There can be no doubt that the concepts of having a pure heart and being merciful are very closely related, and perhaps we should see the arrangement here as inconsequential. However, since the order of the Beatitudes seems to be so purposeful, I believe there may be a reason that this one appears where it does.

To address this I must be personal. After we have shown acts of mercy, what is the temptation we may face? I don't know about you, but after being generous or forgiving, I am tempted at times to think about what I have done and how good I have been. This becomes particularly true when I am praised for the mercy I have shown. It is important in these moments to keep my heart open before God and others, so that he can purify it and keep me serving with right motives. I believe it is very possible that Jesus placed this beatitude here as a reminder that even after we have been reconciled to God and even after we have begun to show his qualities to others, it is necessary to do a heart check to make sure that we do not begin to take the credit for what his grace is producing in us.[10]

## The Peacemakers

I can remember very well the words of President Jimmy Carter as he met with Anwar Sadat of Egypt and Manachem Begin of Israel when the two signed the Camp David Accords on September 17, 1978. He quoted Matthew 5:9: "Blessed are the peacemakers, for they will be called sons of God." I will always remember his comment because I had just finished a serious study of the Sermon on the Mount. Only a few weeks earlier I had taught a class in which I had pointed out that this statement could not be isolated from the other beatitudes. Jesus had a mission of bringing people to peace with God and to peace with other people. Those things only happen *in the kingdom of God*. Only in the kingdom of God do people beat their swords into plowshares (Isaiah 2:4). Only in the kingdom of God do natural enemies live together in peace (Isaiah 11:1–9). But the kingdom is found only when people have embraced the other kingdom attitudes we have been examining.

We can negotiate a measure of peace in the world, but there is no peace with depth unless there is first peace with God. There will be no peace with God until we come to be poor in spirit, to mourn over our sin, to be meek and to hunger and thirst for God's righteousness. I cannot help thinking how interesting it would have been to have had a discussion of this nature with the presidents of Israel, Egypt and the United States. It is hard to imagine President Carter confronting his two guests with the need to admit their poverty of spirit or to mourn over their sin.

What we must understand about this beatitude is that it is just as necessary as the others. As Jesus was sent by God into the world to reconcile the world to himself, so we have been sent into the world to call others to peace with God. If we have been filled with his righteousness, we will have the same passion to see others come to God that we see in Jesus. Those who accept this call will be risking their lives, as we will see shortly, and perhaps this is why God so highly esteems them. What is the blessing they will receive? "They will be called sons of God." They may suffer for their efforts, but God will never leave them; they will be treated as his family, both now and forevermore.[11]

## The Persecuted

Jesus obviously did not have a very good PR person. Such a person would have told him that you don't want to end this series on a negative note. The Beatitudes conclude with these words:

> "Blessed are those who are persecuted because of righteousness,
> for theirs is the kingdom of heaven.

> "Blessed are you when people insult you, persecute you and falsely say all kinds of evil against you because of me. Rejoice and be glad, because great is your reward in heaven, for in the same way they persecuted the prophets who were before you." (Matthew 5:10–12)

Having described the uncommon heart and attitudes the kingdom person will have, Jesus ends on a note of pure realism. If you live like this, people will not like it. Ironically, I suspect it is particularly the peacemaker part that will get us into the most trouble. Most people would be fine if we would

practice our own relationship with God and live our own separate lives in humility before him. But that seventh beatitude
is where the rub comes. It is when a kingdom person goes
forth to call others to the kingdom that the offense occurs.

There is a certain irony in the fact that being a peacemaker is what will get you hated, abused, maybe even killed.
Jesus was the Prince of Peace. He came to reconcile people to
God. Later he would say, "If they persecuted me, they will
persecute you also" (John 15:20). Most people just don't want
to be disturbed. But there are open hearts out there and in
order to find them, we have to go to all kinds of people. We
must trust that God will be with us and rejoice that we have
found the kingdom—regardless of how others may treat us.[12]

Jesus taught attitudes of the kingdom that are not natural.
They are produced only through interaction with God. It
would seem that Jesus placed these attitudes at the forefront
of his message because being a kingdom person is not, first of
all, what you *do,* but it is who you *are.* Jesus did not call people to "do" but to "be." The Beatitudes describe people who
see who they are, who see their need for God and who are
being changed on the inside. As we will observe in the next
chapter, such people have impact in the world.

# 9
# The Kingdom Lifestyle

Philip Yancey writes about a friend of his who taught at a major university in a part of the country where the Bible is often held in high regard. When she assigned an essay for students to write their reactions to the Sermon on the Mount, she was taken aback by what she read. For the most part, they found it full of unreasonable expectations. Some shared that it made them feel very uncomfortable. One student described it as stupid and inhuman.[1] These reactions are probably to be preferred over those who pay lip service to the greatness of the message, but then ignore it in everyday life. The students' candid reactions clearly show that the kingdom lifestyle that Jesus taught about is dramatically unlike what most people think of as a healthy way of life. Even those who are more charitable have found it to contain a utopian message that could not be seriously practiced.

Such thinking misses the mark at several points. First, there is a failure to understand the greatness of the kingdom. The teachings we find in this sermon can only be appreciated in the context of the amazing intrusion of the kingdom into our world. As C. H. Dodd points out, since the kingdom is here, it is no time for a nice "practical morality."[2] Something so different has come that a radically different way of living is called for.

Second, there is a failure to see that the sermon is not a code of law, but a vision of a high calling. We spent an entire chapter on the eight short statements that serve as the beginning of this sermon—it was important to see that what we are dealing with here is primarily a change of attitude and heart. The new attitude is one that no longer asks, "What is the law because I don't want to break it?" No, it is one that says, "I was lost and now I am found. Show me the way to the best and the highest, and I will seek that with all my heart."

Third, there is a failure to see clearly *the One* who gives the call to this lifestyle. What we find in the Sermon on the Mount is a call to be with Jesus, to follow him and to enjoy a relationship with our *Abba,* Father. Outside of that context, these are impossible principles that do make people, like the previously mentioned university students, just feel bad about themselves. A call to be perfect is a burden if we don't see it as a dream of imitating our Father in heaven and the way he has so generously loved us. But the kingdom is great. And this is a call to soar higher and farther.

Finally, this is all about being with God, who is extravagantly generous. Therefore, we can say the Sermon on the Mount is very much for us. The man who knew how to live, Jesus, is very much on the mark in this message.

But a word of caution is in order. Keep in mind how this sermon begins. The attitudes at the beginning are far and away the most important qualities. To use a modern parable, there were once two men named Alex and Ben. Where these men lived, there was a certain crucial attitude needed for a fulfilling life called simply "Heart." In this world where the two men lived, there were ten spiritual facts that everyone was asked to learn. Now as it turned out, Alex had superior intellect and he was able to master the ten key spiritual facts. He knew them well and could discuss them and describe the history of the debates about each of the ten. Ben was not as intellectually skilled as Alex. He was able to only learn three of the spiritual facts. But Ben had Heart and Alex did not. Which man do you suppose was better off? The answer, of course, is Ben. While Alex had more of the truth in his head, his lack of Heart prevented him from making the best use of that truth. Ben had much more to learn, but his right attitude enabled him to use what he did know and gave him the basis for learning more. In the meantime his spirit and his heart served him well and pointed others in the right direction.

When we come to the Sermon on the Mount, the crucial thing is attitude. There may be certain specifics here in this sermon that we will wrestle with throughout our lives, but we must not lose our gratitude or joy about being brought to the kingdom and given the opportunity to show the kingdom to the world. If we stay with the kingdom attitudes, the kingdom lifestyle will come.

It may be helpful to look at the Sermon on the Mount in six parts:

1. Matthew 5:1–12      Different attitudes
2. Matthew 5:13–16     Different effect
3. Matthew 5:17–6:18   Different righteousness
4. Matthew 6:19–34     Different priority
5. Matthew 7:1–12      Different relationship
6. Matthew 7:13–27     Different judgment

This is not the only possible way of organizing this material, but hopefully it will be of some value in helping us focus on Jesus' message. In the previous chapter, we looked at the different attitudes that open the sermon. In the rest of this chapter, we will look at the other five sections.

## Different Effect (Matthew 5:13-16)

> "You are the salt of the earth. But if the salt loses its salti-ness, how can it be made salty again? It is no longer good for anything, except to be thrown out and trampled by men.
> "You are the light of the world. A city on a hill cannot be hidden. Neither do people light a lamp and put it under a bowl. Instead they put it on its stand, and it gives light to everyone in the house. In the same way, let your light shine before men, that they may see your good deeds and praise your Father in heaven." (Matthew 5:13–16)

With two vivid images that everyone can understand, Jesus teaches that people of the kingdom will have an effect on the world. Just as salt and light make a difference because they are different from the elements that they penetrate, the kingdom attitudes Jesus just taught will have impact on the world.

Salt was primarily a preservative which, when rubbed into meat, for example, would stop the decay. Jesus says kingdom people are like that. As they penetrate society, some may per-secute them, but others will be influenced by them and through the message, come also to share in the kingdom. Paul would later write to a disciple about this very influence: "Watch your life and doctrine closely," he said. "Persevere in them, because if you do, you will save both yourself and your hearers" (1 Timothy 4:16).

Light, of course, penetrates into and obliterates the darkness. It illuminates and enables us to find our way and gain direction. Those who are humble, who take sin seriously, who are teachable and who desire righteousness will bring light where there is darkness. Because of them others will see. Most of us who are disciples today are indebted to someone who lived with kingdom attitudes and brought salt and light into our lives. Now we can make the same difference for others.

As Jesus made clear earlier, we should expect opposition. Kingdom attitudes and the kingdom lifestyle will be opposed, but that opposition just gives kingdom people another opportunity to show how different they are from the world around them. Shortly Jesus will even teach about loving enemies.

When I was in Galilee several years ago, near to the place where this sermon would have been delivered, I was struck by how remote it is. You wouldn't think that something that could affect the whole world would start in a place like that. But Jesus tells a little band of mostly lower-class Jews, all from the wrong part of their own little country, that with the right attitudes of the kingdom, they will make a lasting difference in the world. And they did. Two thousand years later, we are still talking about them and being influenced by their lives and words. And these kingdom attitudes are no less powerful today. Those who live by them will be salt and light to a world of people in need.

## Different Righteousness

> "For I tell you that unless your righteousness surpasses that of the Pharisees and the teachers of the law, you will certainly not enter the kingdom of heaven." (Matthew 5:20)

This section of Jesus' sermon runs from Matthew 5:17–6:18, but the key statement is the one above. The religious elite of Jesus' day worked at being righteous, but their concept of righteousness had become superficial. Among the majority, righteousness had to do with correct knowledge of facts and correct outward performance of certain acts; and the scribes and Pharisees spent hours learning the facts, doing the right things. They were much like Alex in the parable we looked at earlier.

Some who first heard these words from Jesus may have thought he was saying they needed to memorize more Scripture than the Pharisees, go more often to the temple, spend more hours in prayer or give another tithe above and beyond the gift they had already given. I heard a Christian comment on this verse and suggest that disciples should fast at least three times a week, to go beyond what the Pharisees did. But right here in the shadow of the Beatitudes, we can be very sure that Jesus was not telling his disciples to outdo the Pharisees in these outward ways.

What we see in this section of the sermon is that there must be a different righteousness of the heart. It will be a righteousness that comes *from God* and is given to those who are poor in spirit and who admit that on their own they have no righteousness at all. The problem with the scribes and Pharisees was not that they were not *doing* enough—they were religious overachievers. The problem was that their righteousness, if we want to call it that, issued from themselves and not from a dependence on God.[3]

In this section, Jesus makes the point that he has not come in opposition to the Torah or the prophets. He has not come to teach people to disregard the law. He has the highest regard for the Scriptures. What he has come to do is to see that the truth is written on people's hearts and they have a righteousness that goes far beyond the observance of any written code.

What follows next are examples of how a person with the new attitudes of the kingdom will respond in different situations (Matthew 5:21–6:18). Let me say two things before we look at some of these. First, I believe we would make a huge mistake if we see these as more things to put on a to-do list so we can out-perform the Pharisees. Rather, it would seem that these are but examples of how to *apply* the new attitudes. Jesus could have given a much more extensive list, but that was not the point. Second, I do not believe these things can possibly make sense to someone who has not taken on the new attitudes we have already looked at. I think this explains the angry reaction of the university students we mentioned at the beginning and the head shaking from many throughout the centuries. They cannot make sense of what Jesus is saying because they do not have the kingdom attitudes and they have not received the blessings that come from those attitudes. If at any point we find ourselves thinking that Jesus is just missing it here or there, our greatest need may not be to wrestle more with the text, but to wrestle more with our hearts. I find that if I am struggling with something in the Sermon on the Mount, I am most helped by returning to the Beatitudes.

In the last part of Matthew 5 and first part of Matthew 6, Jesus illustrates how the new attitudes will work. While it has been said, "Do not murder," Jesus calls on his disciples to have such a different spirit that they will now avoid even anger and harsh words. To show how important relationships are, Jesus calls his followers to act urgently when someone has something against them. Making peace now becomes so important that one who is worshiping should put his gift down at the altar and go work first on repairing the broken relationship.

Without a different heart, this teaching of Jesus becomes no small burden. Anyone who got to the temple and was ready to offer his gift had gone through quite an ordeal. First, he had likely traveled some distance to get to Jerusalem. He had probably stood in line at the money changers' table and then again to buy the animal to be sacrificed or to have his own animal inspected and approved. He next waited in the crowd for the trumpets to blow, signaling the appropriate time to bring the sacrifices. Imagine that just as he was about to offer his gift, he remembered that his brother has something against him. Jesus says that he should have such a heart for reconciliation that, after all this effort, he will put his gift down and go do what it takes to find his brother and be reconciled. Clearly, for Jesus the external activities of worship would have no meaning if relationships were not honored.

The new righteousness calls us to not only avoid adultery, but to say no to lust. In the Jewish culture of the time, divorce was quite easy for men, and a large school of rabbis believed you could put your wife away for almost any reason. The new attitude of the heart calls for an end to such selfishness and for consideration of what effect all this would have on the wife.

Retaliation has a long history in the Middle East, but Jesus says a person with the new attitude will turn the other cheek and go the second mile. Both of these had to be a surprise to his hearers, but the second was particularly shocking. The occupying Roman army could require a Jew to carry a burden for one mile. Each time this happened, it was particularly galling and stirred the Jews' desire to throw the Romans out. The radical righteousness of the kingdom means disciples would volunteer for a second mile, and since this righteousness is all about attitude, we know it would have to be done without resentment or bitterness. That Jesus was willing to teach such a thing in the politically and emotionally charged atmosphere in Galilee speaks volumes about how confident he was about who he was and about this new way.

Jesus' last example in this series was to go far beyond the common idea about how to relate to neighbors and enemies. "Love your enemies," said Jesus, "and pray for those who persecute you" (Matthew 5:44). Luke tells us that on another occasion Jesus went on to say that we should lend to our enemies and not expect anything back (Luke 6:35). Unless you have a whole new understanding of how the extravagant generosity of God is breaking into our world, this will sound like foolishness. But the kingdom gives us a new set of eyes, and we no longer look at life in the normal ways.

In Matthew 5, I am convinced Jesus is not giving us an extensive new law code. He is giving us examples of how the new attitude of the heart will make a difference. From time to time in life we will come to situations about which there is no clear word in Scripture. In such situations we have basically two options. We can say, "I can do what I want to do here because the Scriptures don't give me a rule." On the other hand, we can say, "There is no clear word here, but I want to do something consistent with the attitudes that Jesus says kingdom people will have." Shortly, Jesus will tell us that when we seek such things, we will find them.

In the first part of Matthew 6, Jesus stresses that the kingdom person no longer does spiritual acts for recognition or for the praise of men. Nothing is more inconsistent with the kingdom of the Servant King than ostentatiousness. What we do must be done simply to please God. The religious leaders of his day had a way of making sure that they had a good audience for their "performances"—their praying, their fasting and their giving of alms. They had not come to the poverty of spirit in which we see that "all our righteous acts are like filthy rags" (Isaiah 64:6) and that "nothing good lives in [us], that is, in [our] sinful nature" (Romans 7:18). In contrast with this theatrical religion, kingdom people are not to focus on the praise they will get from men, but on the amazing acceptance they have already been granted by God.

## Different Priority

> "But seek first his kingdom and his righteousness, and all these things will be given to you as well." (Matthew 6:33)

The verse above is the key statement in this next section, the last half of Matthew 6, which focuses on living with a different priority. Again, it is my belief that most everything in the Sermon on the Mount can be traced back to the Beatitudes, and here I would focus your attention on the fourth beatitude. There, Jesus calls us to hunger and thirst for righteousness, to make the pursuit of God's will the overriding passion of our lives. This section of Matthew 6 would seem to be just an elaboration on that idea.

Jesus first challenges us to look at where we locate our treasure. If our treasure—that is, what we really value—is found in this world, then that is where our hearts will be. He calls, instead, for his followers to locate their treasure in heaven where the vicissitudes of life cannot touch it. A kingdom person is one who has decided that there is no treasure on earth that compares with embracing God's kingdom and his righteousness. This is the pearl of great price. This is what you sell everything else to have.

Jesus next talks about our eyes. The priority we have will determine how we see things. "If your eyes are good," he says, "your whole body will be full of light. But if your eyes are bad, your whole body will be full of darkness" (Matthew 6:22–23). If we have located our treasure in the wrong place, we will tend to see everything through a bad set of eyes. We will make judgments and decisions that are harmful because our perspective and our view are all wrong. How often have some of us who counsel others seen this happen? But if we have truly put "first things" first, then we will be able to sort things out and make good decisions, even when life gets complicated.

Then Jesus specifically turns to the issue of money, and says, "No one can serve two masters....You cannot serve God and Money" (Matthew 6:24). If we make money our priority, it will become our master. It will rule us and color our view of life. It will choke out our love for the kingdom. It will destroy our relationship with God. We all must make money (or at least somebody must make money for our support), but money is a dangerous thing. The kingdom person is not one who will live in fear of money, but one who will have such passion for the kingdom of God that money stands no chance of having mastery over him.

Finally, Jesus looks at the basic needs of life—having something to eat, to drink and to wear—and he says if our priority is right, if we seek first the kingdom and God's righteousness, all of these needs will be met because we have a Father in heaven who knows exactly what is required and how to supply it. When our eyes are good, it will make perfectly good sense to seek the kingdom above all else, because there we find the generosity of God.

## Different Relationship

In Matthew 7, after speaking first about having a generous attitude toward other people and their faults, Jesus turns to the different relationship that we enjoy with God in the kingdom. He encourages us to do something that is a real key to living out the kingdom lifestyle described in this sermon: "Ask and it will be given to you; seek and you will find; knock and the door will be opened to you. For everyone who asks receives; he who seeks finds; and to him who knocks, the door will be opened" (Matthew 7:7–8). It is most important to keep all this asking and seeking and knocking in the context of this sermon. Given what we have just seen about priority, we know the kingdom person will not come asking for wealth, luxury and earthly success. Instead, he or she will be asking for such things as a pure heart, the ability to love enemies or the courage to be a real peacemaker.

It is in this context that Jesus brings up the "much more of the heavenly Father" that we looked at back in chapter 7. In our relationship with God we will find that as we hunger and thirst for righteousness and as we long for more of the will of God and power of God to do his will, he will freely and abundantly give. Those who despair about living the Sermon on the Mount seem to ignore this different relationship and the power it brings. Sure, these teachings reveal our inadequacy, but they also reveal a God who is more than adequate, and one who is eager to be faithful.

In my study of this sermon and my efforts to live by it, I find a very important connection between these verses and the opening beatitude. In the first beatitude I am saying that I cannot live this message on my own. In Matthew 7:7–8 I'm being told that I'm not expected to—but I will have a relationship with the Father that will meet my needs.

Interestingly, the last verse in this section contains what we usually call the Golden Rule: "So in everything, do to others what you would have them do to you, for this sums up the Law and the Prophets" (Matthew 7:12). I find it significant that on either side of the words about our relationship with the Father who gives "much more," are instructions about treating other people just as graciously. Jesus will not let us get away from the fact the kingdom is not just about a vertical relationship with God, but also horizontal relationships with others. As one of Jesus' disciples would later write, "For anyone who does not love his brother, whom he has seen, cannot love God, whom he has not seen" (1 John 4:20).

## Different Judgment

The last section of the sermon is not so much about the lifestyle of those in the kingdom as it is about the results of accepting or not accepting the invitation to participate in it. Several things stand out in these verses (Matthew 7:13–29).

First, it is clear that the way of the kingdom is a narrow road (Matthew 7:13–14). It is eminently possible to travel it because God will faithfully support us, but the vast majority will either not trust him or will be too consumed with their own agenda. They will choose the ease of the wide gate and broad road, which does not constrict them or demand too much of them. For a time, this choice might seem to be a good one, but in the end, Jesus says, it leads to destruction. The narrow road of the kingdom, on the other hand, leads to life.

Second, Jesus was not naive. He preached about a generous God, but he still recognized the evil in man. "Watch out,"
he said, "for false prophets" (Matthew 7:15). He went on to say
that many of them look harmless enough, but are like wolves
in sheep's clothing. Using another metaphor, he told us to
check out their fruit, for a bad tree cannot bear good fruit.

Third, Jesus declared that final judgment belongs to him
and will be based on how people respond to what he taught.
We noted at the very beginning of this book how shocking his
words would have been. Those who hear his words and do
not put them into practice will be like a man who built his
house on sand. Those who claim to have been his followers
and claim to have done things in his name, but never had his
heart or the attitudes of the kingdom, will find their religious
houses collapsing. Those who hear his words and put them
into practice will be like the man who builds his house on a
rock. The rain will come down in torrents. The wind will
howl. The waters will rise. But that house will stand. The
lifestyle of the kingdom will be shown to be life to the full.

Something as great as the kingdom of God leads to a
whole new perspective. A new perspective leads to new attitudes. New attitudes lead to a new life. You are not likely to
learn about this life at the Harvard Business School, on Wall
Street or on a playground in Philadelphia. It will not be advo-
cated in the pages of *Time*, *Vogue* or *Sports Illustrated*. It is not
going to be glamorized by Hollywood. But it is still as true
now as when the unlikely man from Nazareth proclaimed it,
and it still takes courage to live it.

# 10
# Conflict and Controversy

As I was leaving my office the day before this chapter was written, a fairly young Christian stopped to talk with me. We reflected on a film we had seen depicting the crucifixion, and then he asked, "How could someone so full of love have been so hated?" His question was similar to one raised many years ago by the famous Bible expositor William Barclay. In *The Mind of Jesus,* he wrote:

> When we read the Gospels, it is very difficult for us to understand the implacable hostility and the envenomed hatred which could not rest until they had driven Jesus to the cross. We find it almost impossible to understand why anyone who lived a life of such love and service and kindness and sympathy should have incurred such savage opposition.

From one perspective these questions are understandable, but they also reflect a certain naive attitude that thinks that the world will appreciate godly people. If Jesus was bringing the kingdom of light into a world of darkness, can we really expect for there not to have been a major reaction? As long as you are friendly and nice, most people will be quite tolerant of you (so long as they are not racists and nationalists and you are not in the wrong group). However, when what you do begins to expose them and begins to reveal their need for change, trouble begins.

We have already seen in our look at the last two beatitudes that the rub comes when we start showing people that they must be different in order to have peace with God. Jesus certainly loved people—even his enemies—but he loved them enough to tell them the truth. When people can't handle the truth, they strike back.

The clash between the established religious views and those of Jesus plays a major role in the Gospels and certainly becomes a dominant part of the story in the final events. If we are trying to understand Jesus' life, we must look more closely at this conflict and what it may mean for those wanting to follow him today. We can identify several reasons why Jesus' message brought him into conflict with religion.

## New Wine

Those who call for a radically new way of looking at the world are often seen as a threat. Particularly in religious matters, the intransigence is often greater because people feel that divine truth or, perhaps more importantly to them, their own position, is at stake.

Jesus certainly understood that what he was saying was different. In the Sermon on the Mount, we have already noted how he said again and again, "You have heard it said…but I say to you…." While he emphasizes his commitment to the Torah and the prophets, he clearly understands that he is calling people to new thinking. In two analogies that we find in each of the first three Gospels, Jesus makes it clear that there is incompatibility between the kingdom he is bringing and the old ways people are accustomed to. Here is Mark's record of those statements:

"No one sews a patch of unshrunk cloth on an old garment. If he does, the new piece will pull away from the old, making the tear worse. And no one pours new wine into old wineskins. If he does, the wine will burst the skins, and both the wine and the wineskins will be ruined. No, he pours new wine into new wineskins." (Mark 2:21–22)

With these words, Jesus leaves no room for any thoughts of reviving the old system: it was beyond repair. The new wine of his teaching will have to be placed in a new wineskin, that is, a new form. In both of the metaphors, the result of trying to mix the old and new is a violent one. Surely such a straightforward challenge would have left the established leaders on the defensive. They saw themselves as the proper authorities, leading the people of God and committed to what they believed were all the right forms. Jesus was obviously calling the people to something that was outside those forms, and as such, was dangerous.

## Prophetic Preaching

The early twentieth century view of Jesus from various liberal writers was of a Jesus meek and mild. When we have the proper understanding of "meek," Jesus was that, but most of those writers did not have such an understanding. They described a Jesus who was the ultimate nice person and was never offensive. But they were not paying attention. "Jesus was not," in Philip Yancey's words, "the bland well-adjusted popular citizen."[2] No, he was a prophet, and prophets have a reputation for being downright offensive.

Prophets of God speak out against injustice, hypocrisy and sham. They call sin by its right name. They show no favoritism. They show great intolerance with legalism and with a fixation on minutiae. Jesus did all this. He minced no words. He did not fall victim to that malady that leads one to "almost say something." His hearers had no doubt about what he felt about the religion of his day. His predecessor, John the Baptist, certainly held nothing back (see Matthew 3:1–10). While Jesus may have had a different style from John, his words were just as pointed. All the mystery of why Jesus was opposed is quickly eliminated when we look at the words he addressed to the religious leaders that we find in just one chapter, Matthew 23:

1.  He condemned them because they preached one thing and practiced another (v3).

2.  He indicted them because they put heavy loads on people but did not lift a finger to help them (v4).

3.  He said everything they did was done for show (v5).

4.  He declared that their behavior in effect blocked the entrance to the kingdom and kept others from entering (v13).

5.  He exposed the spiritual blindness that was involved in making ridiculous rules about swearing that were designed to be manipulated for personal gain (vv16–22).

6.  He condemned them for picking and straining at some fine points of religion while neglecting the great principles of justice, love and faithfulness (vv23–24).

7.  He rebuked them for their emphasis on outward show and their lack of emphasis on inward change (vv25–28).

8.  He indicted them for having the same attitude as those
    who killed the prophets while claiming to honor them
    (vv29–30).

Referring to these leaders, Jesus repeatedly uses the Greek
word *hupokrites*. Used centuries before to describe someone
who memorized an epic poem and could recite it for a public
gathering, the word was eventually used to describe an actor,
one who played a role on the stage. It eventually came to be
used in a more negative sense to describe a pretender. This is
the worst possible thing that could be said about a religious
leader.

I find that there is a side of me that gets a kick out of how
Jesus went after these people, but I am not sure my feelings
are altogether righteous. There is another side of me, probably a better side, that wants to understand why a man who
preached love for enemies and turning the other cheek,
would speak so bluntly to these authorities. When you are
calling someone a hypocrite and a blind guide, there doesn't
seem to be a lot of love involved. Why was Jesus talking to
these people in this way?

If we look closely at the prophetic tradition, we find that
the prophets were men who saw clearly the holiness of God.
They found almost nothing as offensive to the holy God as
men who thought they could pretend about where their real
affections lay. Such spiritual frauds often found their way into
positions of leadership and thus had the opportunity to infect
others with their deceitful hearts. Because God loves his people and wants them all to see his truth, he cannot stand by
and watch as his life-giving message is being contaminated
and ruined, and people are being misled. Because God's

prophets have caught God's heart, neither can they. Ungodly religion must be strongly rebuked. God's displeasure with empty and deceptive religion must be declared. At such times nice words will not drive the point home. To cite Jeremiah, when "a horrible and shocking thing has happened in the land" (Jeremiah 5:30), people must be shaken to their senses. Too much is at stake.

True prophets proclaim God's judgment with heavy hearts. Certainly, Jesus did (Matthew 23:37). He did not get some emotional high from exposing false religion. He wept over a city where people honored God with their lips while their hearts were far from him (Luke 19:41). He wanted them all to receive God's generosity, and he cried over those whose attitudes were too hardened to receive it. Anyone who enjoys scorching others for their hypocrisy has some serious personal soul searching to do.

None of us will ever again have the authority that Jesus had to speak as he did. Yet, there will be an ongoing need to bring the word of God to bear on people's lives and declare that not everyone who says, "Lord, Lord," is really doing the Father's will. Like the Old Testament prophets who came before Jesus, his followers today will need to confess that they are not qualified to be prophets. At the same time, they must stand in grace and be filled with the Spirit, not holding back from speaking what they know to be true.

## Traditions That Tumbled

Some of the opposition to Jesus was engendered by his attitude toward the highly esteemed traditions the Jews were so committed to. Judaism in the first century put great weight on the traditions of the elders. With a desire not to break the laws of the Torah or even come close to doing so, they had developed layers of tradition. Obedience to these rules was held to be necessary for righteousness. "Why," some of the Pharisees asked Jesus, "do your disciples break the tradition of the elders? They don't wash their hands before they eat!" (Matthew 15:2). They were not talking here about matters of health, but rather, the ceremonial washing that the traditions prescribed. The keeping of the traditions was at the heart of their spirituality. Jesus came along and seemingly paid them no regard.

In his discussion with them about this matter, he does more than ignore these rules. "And why do you break the command of God for the sake of your tradition?" he asked them (Matthew 15:3). Not only was Jesus not committed to their traditions, but he drew a sharp contrast between them and the commands of God. He quotes Isaiah, who spoke of worship that is done in vain because the teachings are just rules made by men (Matthew 15:9, Isaiah 29:13).

The Pharisees and their predecessors made the mistake repeated a thousand times over in history. They created forms and rules that made them feel spiritual. They put those rules in a box and drew their security from obeying them. Jesus' words identify the real problem here: "made by man." There is a world of difference in something originating from God and something originating from man. All of us who have been involved in any organized (or even disorganized) form of religion have probably given allegiance to some traditions of men. Jesus would teach us to examine these very carefully, first, to make sure that they are not in opposition to truth from God, and second, so we will not gain security or reassurance from things that pass away.

## Of Sin and Sinners

As people often are, the religious leaders in Jesus' day were a study in contradiction. On the one hand they sought to avoid contact with "sinners." On the other hand they did not take sin seriously enough. Jesus clashed with them on both points.

Unlike the average rabbi, Jesus often was found with undesirables, people of questionable character and "disreputable folk" (Mark 2:15, Phillips). Roundly criticized and discredited for this (Matthew 9:11, Luke 7:39), he insisted that associating with people who recognized their need was at the heart of his mission.

> On hearing this, Jesus said, "It is not the healthy who need a doctor, but the sick. But go and learn what this means: 'I desire mercy, not sacrifice.' For I have not come to call the righteous, but sinners." (Matthew 9:12–13)

> "For the Son of Man came to seek and to save what was lost." (Luke 19:10)

The goal of the religious leaders seemed to be to protect their personal purity (external though it was). Jesus' goal was to reach out to the impure and to help them find healing and redemption. In view of this, William Barclay wrote:

> There can be no common ground between a religion which sees the sinner as a man to be avoided at all costs and religion which sees the sinner as a man to be sought at all costs, between a religion which sees the sinner as a man to be destroyed and a religion which sees the sinner as a man to be saved.[3]

That these religious authorities saw themselves as too good to associate with sinners speaks volumes about how deceived they were about their own hearts. Perhaps a few of them got some glimpse into themselves during the incident with the woman taken in adultery that we looked at in chapter 7, but for the most part, they failed to see that their own need was as great as that of all other men.

What Jesus' critics didn't seem to see is that when he associated with sinners, he always did so with a vision, with a plan and with a message. He was not content to just make them comfortable around him. He loved them and called them to a new life. Those who responded understood they were to repent. Those forgiven understood that they were to leave their lives of sin. The goal of the physician is not just to spend time with the sick, but to help them get well. His opponents focused not on his goals or on the outcome of his ministry, but on the fact that he was simply with the wrong people—those whom they had labeled as unrighteous.

Today, it seems to me, we are much more likely to find a different problem. Today many religious leaders have no problem associating with people of all kinds of lifestyles, but they do so without a message to bring to them. There is no inherent virtue in associating with people if we don't have the same goal for them that Jesus had. I remember a man in a group I led many years ago. He boasted that he had lots of contact with sinners and rebuked others who just hung out in their own little Christian ghetto. He was right about them, but what he did had no impact. He hung out with "pagans," but he had no deep convictions and no message that he shared. Ironically, he felt as self-righteous as the Pharisees, for just the opposite reason, and he had the same impact on the lost world as they did.

If the religious leaders clashed with Jesus over his association with sinners, they probably had an even deeper conflict with him when it came to what constituted sin. For all their efforts to avoid sin and sinners, the truth is that they did not take sin seriously enough. Sin for them had to do with breaking various laws and violating external regulations. Sin for Jesus was something much deeper and much more serious. It is found in the heart and must be dealt with at that level. To those focused on the external and the keeping of the right traditions, he said:

> "Don't you see that whatever enters the mouth goes into the stomach and then out of the body? But the things that come out of the mouth come from the heart, and these make a man 'unclean.' For out of the heart come evil thoughts, murder, adultery, sexual immorality, theft, false testimony, slander. These are what make a man 'unclean'; but eating with unwashed hands does not make him 'unclean.'" (Matthew 15:17–20)

Man's problem was much worse than established religion thought it was. It could never be cured by rules and ritual. It was going to take something that got down into the heart where these vile things are found in each of us. All men, including those who see themselves as models of virtue, are really slaves of sin (John 8:31–36). Sin is that pervasive and it is that serious. For those who acknowledged their need in Jesus' day, the gospel became a message of unspeakable joy. For those who wanted to defend their own righteousness, it was a thorn in their sides, and the one who preached it had to be stopped.

## If They Persecuted Me

There is, I suppose, a people-pleasing side of me that would like to tell you that following Jesus is always wonderful. But this is not the message Jesus gave to his disciples, and it is not the one I can give to you today. (There are several reasons why it is not true, and we will look at some of these in chapter 14.) Instead, Jesus promised that his disciples would get the same kind of opposition he got. In other words, there is a price to pay for living the kingdom life in this world.

> "Remember the words I spoke to you: 'No servant is greater than his master.' If they persecuted me, they will persecute you also. If they obeyed my teaching, they will obey yours also." (John 15:20)

When I would teach on this theme a number of years ago in the days of the old Soviet Union, I would ask my listeners to think of an American going to Moscow where he made no bones about his patriotism. I encouraged them to envision this fellow putting his American flag up in his window and starting each day with a high-volume recording of the "Star-Spangled Banner." "What do you suppose would be the reaction?" I asked. Whenever someone lives in one place with an entirely different worldview, there is bound to be conflict and controversy.

Those who follow Jesus have embraced the principles of the kingdom of God, but they remain in this world. They have become citizens of heaven with new loyalties and new priorities, but they live among people who do not share these priorities. Like Jesus, they have a mission to reach out, to speak the good news, but also to tell people *why* they need his message. They must associate with sinners, but call people to change. They must love unconditionally, but live radically—and declare that this is the only way to live. As in Jesus' day, some people will welcome the message, but the majority will not.

In view of this, it is not shocking when followers of Jesus are opposed. Rather, it is shocking when they are not.

Persecution is not something any emotionally balanced disciple ever pursues, but when we pursue righteousness, Jesus makes it clear: persecution will come.

Commenting on Christianity, Sigmund Freud is supposed to have said something about how interesting it is that the God Christians have created is one who says what they always wanted to hear. If he indeed said this, I have often wondered what Bible he was reading. The Jesus we encounter in the Gospels offers us some unbelievably good news, but at the same time, promises us some things we did not really want to hear: following him will mean conflict and controversy. But then some things are worth it. As we will see in the next two chapters, he faced the worst, believing it was more than worth it. And it was.

# 11

# Even Death on a Cross

Jesus began his ministry announcing the kingdom of God. He preached again and again about the invitation God was offering. He called people to change and open their lives to the abundance God wanted to give. He spoke of the joy and gladness those in the kingdom would find. But even in those early days, he must have pondered some of Isaiah's words regarding the Servant. "But he was pierced for our transgressions....He was crushed for our iniquities....He was led like a lamb to the slaughter....He poured out his life unto death" (Isaiah 53:5, 7, 12).

As his ministry progressed, he increasingly had these foreboding prophecies on his mind. Several times in his final weeks or months, he predicted his suffering and death. Luke tells us of three different occasions when Jesus forewarned the disciples (Luke 9:22, 17:25, 22:15). Each time, the disciples seemed resistant, dull or distracted; and they were of little encouragement to him. We can only guess that when he spoke of these impending events during that amazing experience with Moses and Elijah on the Mount of Transfiguration (Luke 9:31), he surely received more support. Apparently, heartened by this encounter, Jesus "resolutely set out for Jerusalem" (Luke 9:51). Though the disciples seemed clueless, they were nonetheless loyal to their leader. As C. H.

Dodd points out, "they steeled themselves for the ordeal, and followed him."[1]

Once in the city, his clash with the establishment intensified and he knew that the time was drawing near. John tells us that he agonized, questioned and counseled himself:

> "Now my heart is troubled, and what shall I say? 'Father, save me from this hour'? No, it was for this very reason I came to this hour." (John 12:27)

In this moment we see both his struggle and his surrender. As one who shared our flesh, he could not discount the trauma he was about to endure. As one committed to the will of God, he could not turn back.

Did he know his death would come by crucifixion? Whether from the Scriptures[2] or through divine foreknowledge, we have to say that he did. He knew the suffering would be severe. He also knew Isaiah 53 spoke of "the suffering of his soul." If he was to be the ransom and the sin offering for the many (Mark 10:45), his physical death would only be part of it. The worst suffering would come from another source.

## The Last Supper

All the Gospels describe a final meal that Jesus had with his disciples. The first three Gospels make it clear that it was the Passover celebration. It is a helpful exercise to try putting yourself in the place of one of the Twelve and to imagine what you would have felt as the events unfolded that night at the feast.

At one point during the meal, Jesus takes the bread and he says: "This is my body." He takes the cup and he says, "This is my blood of the covenant, poured out for many." You have eaten the Passover feast maybe fifteen to twenty times since you were a teenager, but never have you heard anything like this. You have probably eaten the Passover with Jesus before, but now you are hearing him say something totally new and thoroughly strange. I would be surprised if some of them didn't turn to others and ask, "What did he say? Did he say what I thought he said?"

Those of us who are Christians have heard those words many times, but what is familiar to us now had to be a shock to those who were there on that historic night. It is doubtful that any of them understood what he meant. Military people talk about "the fog of war." The disciples were in the fog of the spiritual battle. It was all a confusing blur. We sometimes talk about this event and say Jesus was instituting the Lord's Supper. However, this was probably the last thought on the minds of the Twelve. Sometime later they would reflect on all this, remember it, understand it and appreciate it. That night they were in the dark.

Matthew and Mark tell us the meal ended with the singing of a hymn before they headed for the Mount of Olives, a favorite place for pilgrims to bed down for the night. I have to believe that whatever the hymn was, the disciples just mouthed the words. It was probably the most unenthusiastic singing in the history of the Jesus movement. They were stunned, trying to understand what it was they were in the middle of.

## Gethsemane

If the disciples' confusion at the supper was great, it only got worse on the way to the campsite. First, Jesus gave them the sobering prediction that they would all fall away. When Peter objected and assured Jesus that this would never happen with him, Jesus predicted that with Peter it would actually be worse; he would disown Jesus three times (Mark 14:28–31). The fog and the darkness must have grown thicker.

Once on the Mount of Olives, east of the city across the Kidron Valley, Jesus retreated to an area called Gethsemane. Mark describes a scene heavy with pathos:

> They went to a place called Gethsemane, and Jesus said to his disciples, "Sit here while I pray." He took Peter, James and John along with him, and he began to be deeply distressed and troubled. "My soul is overwhelmed with sorrow to the point of death," he said to them. "Stay here and keep watch." (Mark 14:32–34)

Jesus, at this most difficult moment in his life, was still building community. He was sorrowful and distressed, but he was asking his friends to be with him. He had to know they were not going to be much help, but in the kingdom of God, relationships are vital and must be maintained in all circumstances. Later on, they would remember how he did not choose to go it alone, but to have his friends with him. When faced with tough things, some of us, particularly those of us who are men, would rather handle it by ourselves—it seems less complicated. I have not always been good at asking friends to be with me in my dark hours. Even in this situation at Gethsemane, Jesus is teaching me.

What most of us know about Jesus' time of prayer is that he made an earnest appeal to God in the hope that there might be some way other than the cross before him. If there is any doubt that Jesus fully shared our humanity, it should be dispelled by this scene:

> Going a little farther, he fell to the ground and prayed that if possible the hour might pass from him. "*Abba,* Father," he

> said, "everything is possible for you. Take this cup from me.
> Yet not what I will, but what you will." (Mark 14:35–36)

Jesus is in as mighty a struggle here as a human being can be in. Like a child, he pours out his soul to his *Abba*, Father, seeking some way to resolve an awful dilemma. If nothing changes, his life will become a guilt offering (Isaiah 53:10) and he will bear the sin of many people (Isaiah 53:12); but to do so means he must be cut off from God and feel his own soul suffer the penalty of sin. He declares to his Father what he has preached to others: "Everything is possible with God." This being true, surely there is some other way to resolve this.

"*Abba*," he says. He had never known anything but the deepest fellowship with his *Abba*, his Papa. Surely, there was some way to maintain that relationship and not be cut off, but still save the world. But then his surrender to his Father emerges: "Yet not what I will, but what you will."

In that statement—maybe the most important line in the New Testament—Jesus shows us the heart of the kingdom of God. Those in the kingdom may struggle mightily, but in the end they have one passion: God's will, not their own. Mark tells us that Jesus returned to pray this prayer two more times, and Luke adds that his sweat became as drops of blood (Luke 22:44). Let us never doubt that it was a struggle. But in the end Jesus is resolved. The cross would come the next day, but the battle was won that night in Gethsemane.

Some years ago, I was able to visit this famous grove of olive trees and, from there, look across the valley to the walls of the Old City of Jerusalem. The scene will forever be etched in my mind. The truth is, I need to go there every day—at least in my heart. Life is truly found in saying, "*Abba*, Father,

not my will but yours be done." Jesus did the right thing. He
trusted the Father. We can be thankful that he did.[3]

## The Cross

After a first trial before the Sanhedrin, in which he was
charged with blasphemy, and a second before the Roman
procurator, Pontius Pilate, in which the Jews changed the
charge to treason, Jesus was sentenced to die by crucifixion.
Following a vicious procedure known as scourging (Mark
uses the word "flogged"), there was a routine time for the
soldiers to mock and ridicule the victim. Eventually, Jesus was
forced to carry the cross-beam that he would die on, to a
point outside the city gates. The route from Pilate's quarters in
the Antonia Fortress to the place of crucifixion was purpose-
fully long and drawn out to give more people an opportunity
to consider the dangers of antagonizing the Romans.

Invented by the Persians and perfected by the Romans as
a means of discouraging rebels and runaway slaves, crucifixion produced effects on its victims that have never been
equaled. Thomas Cahill points out that the suffering of Jesus
was so great that it was four centuries before any Christian
dared to portray it in art. From the earliest days of the
Christian movement, Christians created art forms to show
everything from the descending of the Holy Spirit at Jesus'
baptism to the Last Supper. But not one crucifixion scene can
be found.[4] Cahill notes that when the first of these appears in
the fifth century, crucifixion had not been practiced in the
empire for a hundred years. Only after the last of those with
firsthand knowledge of its horrors had died were there artists
who dared to portray the crucifixion.[5]

## The Seven Words

Jesus was the Teacher, and it is remarkable that even from the cross, he continued to teach us how to live. When the four Gospels are combined, we have seven sayings that Jesus uttered from the cross. That a man could say anything intelligible while being crucified is amazing. That we have seven statements, all with great meaning, is all the more powerful.[6]

Since no one writer records all of these statements, we cannot be entirely sure of the order in which they occur, but we will examine them according to what appears most likely.

### *"Forgive Them"*

> Jesus said, "Father, forgive them, for they do not know what they are doing." And they divided up his clothes by casting lots. (Luke 23:34)

Isaiah had written that the Servant would make intercession for the transgressors (Isaiah 53:12). While this entire event can be viewed as a fulfillment of this prophecy, it is most interesting that apparently Jesus' first words from the cross were a prayer for those who were putting him there. "His hands can no longer perform acts of love for friend or enemy," wrote Oswald Sanders. "His feet can no more carry him on acts of mercy. But one form of ministry, the highest, is still open to him. He can still pray."[7] And he chooses not to pray for himself but for others. He is the Servant.

As we have seen so clearly, the extravagant grace of God had been a major theme in his message. Now we see another powerful expression of this. Jesus' heart is to extend grace and forgiveness to those who are doing him harm. "Love your enemies, and pray for them," he had taught; and to the last, he lived that message. In so doing, he teaches us still.

*"Here Is Your Mother"*

> When Jesus saw his mother there, and the disciple whom he loved standing nearby, he said to his mother, "Dear woman, here is your son," and to the disciple, "Here is your mother." From that time on, this disciple took her into his home. (John 19:26–27)

If the first statement brought to mind a great theme that was consistently preached throughout his ministry and one that fulfilled the words written by a prophet hundreds of years before, this one brings us to a very local and personal situation we can all relate to. The relationship of mother and child is a special one. Jesus may be bringing the fulfillment of the ages, but when Mom is there, she needs his attention. Jesus was on a divine mission and was painfully accomplishing it. But there was the woman who had given him birth, who had changed his diapers, who had worried over him as a preteen, who had followed him with doubts, but had stayed with him to the very end, even when some of the Twelve had deserted him. In what must have been an hour of great distress for them both, he cared for her.

"Dear woman" may sound somewhat impersonal to us, but in the Jewish culture these were the words of courtesy and deep respect. He addresses her warmly and assures her that there will be one to protect her and provide for her after he is gone. Relationships are what matter, and Jesus was attentive to this most special relationship under extremely trying circumstances.

*"With Me in Paradise"*

> One of the criminals who hung there hurled insults at him: "Aren't you the Christ? Save yourself and us!"
>
> But the other criminal rebuked him. "Don't you fear God," he said, "since you are under the same sentence? We are punished justly, for we are getting what our deeds deserve. But this man has done nothing wrong."
>
> Then he said, "Jesus, remember me when you come into your kingdom."
>
> Jesus answered him, "I tell you the truth, today you will be with me in paradise." (Luke 23:39–43)

When I read this account, I think immediately of the parable Jesus told in Matthew 20 about the landowner and the workers in his vineyard. To the amazement of those who had worked all day and were paid exactly what they were told they would be paid, the landowner gave the same wages to one who did not join the workforce until the end of the day. The parable ends with these words: "Don't I have the right to do what I want with my own money? Or are you envious because I am generous?" (Matthew 20:15). Here is a common criminal, at a point in time when he can do nothing to make up for his wrongs and cannot contribute even one hour of service to the work of God. Is it possible that he can be completely forgiven and enjoy the same blessings in eternity as one who has served *and suffered for righteousness* for many years? Even if this does not seem to pass our test of fairness, the answer is yes—because God is just that generous. This "insanely generous love" that we have seen and heard about throughout Jesus' ministry is shining through even on this dark Friday.

*"Why Have You Forsaken Me?"*

> From the sixth hour until the ninth hour darkness came over all the land. About the ninth hour Jesus cried out in a loud voice, *"Eloi, Eloi, lama sabachthani?"*—which means, "My God, my God, why have you forsaken me?" (Matthew 27:45–46)

With this statement we come to the most painful moment in the passion of Jesus and surely to the Holy of Holies of the New Testament. The fact that Jesus was quoting from Psalm 22 and was once again fulfilling Scripture does not take anything away from his agony here. It is unlikely we will ever fully know what he felt. It was this moment he had dreaded when he said, "Now my heart is troubled, and what shall I say? 'Father, save me from this hour'?" (John 12:27). It was the anticipation of this moment that caused him to cry, *"Abba,* Father...take this cup from me" (Mark 14:36). He understood like no one else how life is found in a relationship with God (John 17:3). And now Jesus the Servant was pouring his life out unto death (Isaiah 53:12), about to experience complete separation from his Father.

If there was this cry of anguish on Earth, what must have been the sound that echoed through heaven? Surely the angels trembled. If we think that God the Father viewed all this stoically, without emotion or expression, we have not seen the Biblical picture of God. He is the God who rejoices over his people with singing (Zephaniah 3:17), the God who runs with joy to meet the prodigal who returns (Luke 15:20), and the God who fills heaven with rejoicing over just one lost soul who is found (Luke 15:10). He is a God who shows his emotions. How did he express those emotions when Jesus cried, "My God, my God, why have you forsaken me?" There are mysteries here too deep for us to penetrate, but it is clear that God the Father and God the Son were going to the depths for us. No pain was too great for God to endure. No price was too high to pay. In the words of a great hymn:

> Were the whole realm of nature mine,
> That were a present far too small;
> Love, so amazing, so divine,
> Demands my soul, my life, my all.

## "I Am Thirsty"

> Later, knowing that all was now completed, and so that the Scripture would be fulfilled, Jesus said, "I am thirsty." (John 19:28)

The words of Jesus from the cross take us back and forth between the fulfillment of a vast eternal plan and the realities of human existence. Life is just that way. I have been given the privilege to sit here and write about the most important events that the world has known, but as I write these words, it is about an hour past my normal lunchtime, and I am hungry. I will have to eat before I can finish this chapter. The mundane intrudes on the majestic. Jesus would understand that.

Jesus was a most unique man. I am persuaded that there has been no one like him. But he was a man. I remember someone saying once that the Gospels never portray him as a Herculean character who walks six inches off the ground. He felt things we feel; he hurt in ways we hurt. Yes, he had a great mission. He went about spreading the good news of the kingdom. He had amazing impact. But he had to eat and drink and sleep. He got tired. He dozed off in a boat. He had to find housing. He had to arrange for a room where he could eat supper with his disciples. In Jesus of Nazareth, the God of the universe came into our world and walked in our shoes. He did not shield himself from life. He did not live above us or apart from us. The Jesus who died there that day was one of us.

An unnamed disciple, who came later with unusually deep insights into the meaning of Jesus' humanity, would write these words:

> For we do not have a high priest who is unable to sympathize with our weaknesses, but we have one who has been tempted in every way, just as we are—yet was without sin. Let us then approach the throne of grace with confidence, so that we may receive mercy and find grace to help us in our time of need. (Hebrews 4:15–16)

## "It Is Finished"

> When he had received the drink, Jesus said, "It is finished." With that, he bowed his head and gave up his spirit. (John 19:30)

John and Luke both give us words of Jesus that were spoken just moments before he died. There is probably no way to know which of these were his final words. But we will consider first the statement: "It is finished." Later writers of the New Testament would reflect on all that Jesus completed. Two thousand years after the fact, theologians are still exploring all that these words mean. But what may have been foremost in Jesus' mind when he said, "It is finished"?

There can be no doubt that Jesus came seeing himself as the Servant whom Isaiah had promised. He had proclaimed good news to the poor, freedom to the captives and the recovery of sight to the blind (Isaiah 61:1). He had brought comfort to those who mourn (Isaiah 61:2). He had gathered disciples and had laid the foundation for the new Israel; and now, in this final moment, Jesus was becoming the guilt offering (Isaiah 53:10) and bearing the sin of many (Isaiah 53:12). He had done what God had sent him to do. His work as a man was finished. What would happen next would be totally in the hands of God. Just as Isaiah had promised, God would now honor the one who had finished his work. "He will see the light of life and be satisfied" (Isaiah 53:11) and "I will give him a portion among the great" (Isaiah 53:12).

If there were any of his enemies close enough to hear the words Jesus uttered, they may have silently hoped that Jesus himself, along with this nonsense he preached, was all "finished" in quite a different sense. Little did they realize that the seed which falls into the ground and dies produces many seeds (John 12:24).

*"Into Your Hands"*

> Jesus called out with a loud voice, "Father, into your hands I commit my spirit." When he had said this, he breathed his last. (Luke 23:46)

With the words of Psalm 31:5 on his lips, Jesus died. Throughout his life he had been putting himself into the Father's hands, modeling for all of us the way to find real life. To the end, he was talking to his Father. Now as he prepared to face the wrath we all deserve and which he did not, his conviction had not wavered: the Father can be trusted.

We cannot know all that was happening here or all that Jesus would experience between this time and the resurrection (if indeed, we can even speak of "time" in regard to the realms into which he would pass). Whatever was coming, this appears to be a moment of quiet confidence. In my thinking, some unspeakable pain of total separation yet lay ahead, but what he was most focused on were the hands of his Father.

I frequently play a song from a popular artist that speaks of "standing in his presence on holy ground." As I come to the foot of the cross and hear Jesus' last words, this is exactly what I feel. I don't deserve to be here and I don't deserve to get to write about this and attach my name in some way to this story—except as a perpetrator with regard to his pain. With Peter, I say, "Go away, Lord. I am a sinful man" (Luke 5:8). But then I realize he went through all this for me and for you. This was the plan that would allow us to know the Father just as he did.

> What language shall I borrow to thank Thee,
>     dearest Friend,
> For this, Thy dying sorrow, Thy pity without end?
> O make me Thine forever; and should I fainting be,
> Lord, let me never, never, outlive my love to Thee.

# The Empty Tomb

12

Earlier, I suggested that we try to put ourselves in the place of one of the disciples at the Passover meal before Jesus died. I would suggest that we engage in that same exercise again, this time imagining what it would have felt like for one of them after his death. You have just spent three years of your life with someone. You have never known anyone like him. You have never felt personally loved and cared for by anyone the way you felt when you were with him. However, he said things you still don't understand.

At times you were so sure he was the promised Messiah, but then he would say and do things that were maddening. He was never interested in gathering the Jews to evict the Romans. He was more focused on exposing the Jewish establishment. Did he have it all turned around?

Toward the end, events began to move very quickly, and you found your emotions being jerked back and forth. At first there was perplexing talk of suffering and death. However, soon after he spoke of these things, he was welcomed like a king in a joyous reception as he came riding into Jerusalem. But then the mood turned darker. His conflicts with the spiritual leaders intensified. The Passover meal that you ate with him a few days ago was one of the strangest experiences of your life. He seemed perfectly in control, but you and your fellow apostles could not make sense of the strange things he was saying. On the way to a place to spend the night, he told you that you would all fall away and that Peter, the de facto leader of your little group, would disown him three times before the night was over. Weary with confusion, the three who were closest to him kept falling asleep at a place of prayer.

Abruptly there were soldiers with weapons. He was taken. You and the others were intimidated. You fled. You hid. You tried to think. You tried to pray. You probably wept. News came back to you that he had been tried and sentenced to death. How could this be? What had he done that was so bad? You may have even heard the shouts of the crowd as he carried his cross-beam to the place of execution. You were too afraid to venture out. You heard that the women stayed with him and that John came back. A combination of fear, uncertainty and humiliation left you almost paralyzed. What did it all mean? How did it come to this? What are *we* to do now?

The next day it was still the Sabbath. Normally you would have been with Jesus at a synagogue service, but you and the others dared not go out. It was the longest day of your life. The Sabbath ended at sundown. You slept fitfully that night. The morning of the first day of the week started with the others in awkward silence. No one seemed to know what to do or what to say. The word was that some of the women were trying to find the tomb where Jesus' body had been taken. You had a vague feeling you should be doing something, but you were too numb to act.

Suddenly, the silence was broken by the excited voices of Mary Magdalene, Joanna, Mary the mother of James and others with them. You caught only bits and pieces. "The stone was moved." "His body was gone." "Two men." "Shining clothes."

"He is not here." "Raised on the third day." You and the others were too smart to believe these silly women. It was all dismissed as nonsense. But the truth was, everyone's curiosity was aroused. Peter and John decided to make a reconnaissance trip to the tomb. Because you didn't know what else to do with yourself, you agreed to run an errand to the village of Emmaus with one of the others. By the time the day was over, life had changed forever.

The "unreliable" testimony of the women turned out to be true. He was risen! Your friend Thomas missed the first appearance, but when he saw the nail prints, he believed. This didn't help just Thomas, but all of you. You saw him the first time, but you needed more, and thankfully, you saw him again and again. Here was the absolutely amazing thing: in spite of your failures and your confusion and your desertion, he was still smiling at you and telling you how you would be used in the kingdom. And you believed him.

## At the Center of the Faith

Something very much like this must have happened to those early followers of Jesus. The belief in Jesus' resurrection was not, as some would have us believe, an idea that grew as time passed. Careful scholarship has shown that faith in the resurrection was found in the church in its very earliest days. In the words of one scholar:

> In short, the earliest Christianity did not consist of a new doctrine about God nor a new hope of immortality nor even new theological insights about the nature of salvation. It consisted of the recital of a great event, of a mighty act of God: the raising of Christ from the dead.[1]

There was never a time when it was not at the center of the faith. In fact, it was the resurrection that created the church, not the other way around. Without the resurrection there would have never been a church. Without the resurrection, that band of dispirited, disorganized, confused disciples would have wandered back to their separate lives, feeling like failures. But something dramatic and historic happened. Something transformed them. Something put fire in their bellies and passion in their hearts. Something made them bold and fearless. The witness of the Gospels is consistent: this something was nothing less than the bodily presence of the resurrected Jesus.

Luke tells us that the resurrection appearances went on for forty days (Acts 1:3). Sometimes they occurred in a room behind locked doors, sometimes on the road, sometimes by a lake, sometimes at breakfast. Wherever they happened, as C. H. Dodd points out, the appearances had two effects: first, amazement (and sometimes doubt), and then overwhelming certainty. "They were dead sure," he says, "that they had met Jesus."[2] A quick survey of the opening chapters of Acts reveals that they simply could not stop talking about the resurrection:

> "For one of these must become a witness with us of his resurrection." (Acts 1:22)

> "But God raised him from the dead, freeing him from the agony of death, because it was impossible for death to keep its hold on him." (Acts 2:24)

> "God has raised this Jesus to life, and we are all witnesses of the fact." (Acts 2:32)

> "You killed the author of life, but God raised him from the dead. We are witnesses of this." (Acts 3:15)

"When God raised up his servant, he sent him first to you to bless you by turning each of you from your wicked ways." (Acts 3:26)

They were greatly disturbed because the apostles were teaching the people and proclaiming in Jesus the resurrection of the dead. (Acts 4:2)

"Then know this, you and all the people of Israel: It is by the name of Jesus Christ of Nazareth, whom you crucified but whom God raised from the dead, that this man stands before you healed." (Acts 4:10)

With great power the apostles continued to testify to the resurrection of the Lord Jesus, and much grace was upon them all. (Acts 4:33)

"The God of our fathers raised Jesus from the dead— whom you had killed by hanging him on a tree." (Acts 5:30)

They preached Christ crucified and the wisdom and power of the cross, but this would have never happened had they not been certain about the resurrection. God was at work in his surprising ways in the dark events of the cross, but this would never have been believed, nor should it have been, without the resurrection. The cross was the supreme expression of love. The resurrection was the supreme proof that the cross was really of God. The cross and resurrection belong together in the redemptive plan. Apart from the resurrection, the cross is just another tragedy. Apart from the cross, the resurrection would have been just another miracle. But because the resurrection was the return of the Lamb of God who had just given himself for the world, it has life-changing consequences for every one of us.

So, did it really happen? There were no video cameras rolling on that morning of the first day of the week. If you demand that kind of evidence, I cannot help you. However, look at the accounts of the resurrection in the context of the life of an amazing man who made startling claims and taught extraordinary things. Look at them in the context of his message, that the power of God was breaking into our world. Take into account the Old Testament scriptures that were being fulfilled by what he did. Somewhere in this, include the fact that the tomb was empty. Then add to the picture the utter transformation of a bunch of bumpkins from Galilee, who all said their change came for one reason: they saw the resurrected Jesus. Look at the fact that after these events you could not shut them up, intimidate them or kill enough of them to stop the spread of their message.

When you put it all together in one big picture, the evidence is thoroughly compelling. As hard as it was for first century people to believe and as hard as it is for modern men and women to believe, there is just nothing else that makes sense of all the facts. He came out of the tomb.

## What Does It Mean?

It is one thing to say that the resurrection happened and that the evidence for it is abundant, but what does it mean? We have said that this is a book about how to live. What does the resurrection have to do with that? What follows is not a complete list, but here are several things the resurrection means and how it makes a difference in the lives of those who become disciples.

First, the resurrection means that Jesus is vindicated and can be fully trusted. It was remarkable that a seemingly sane man could grow up in the Jewish culture, be devoted to the Torah and attend the synagogue services—and yet say the things he said. The people had met no one like him. His teachings were fresh, pointed and full of new depth. His touch was full of compassion. But if the crucifixion had been the end, he would have been just another enigmatic figure of history and his teachings would have become the stuff of some arcane doctoral dissertation.

But the resurrection meant that an exclamation point, not a question mark, was put at the end of his life. Jesus had said that he was the way, the truth and the life and that no man could come to the Father except through him. As outrageous as that would have sounded, we now know it is true. He had taught things that ran clearly against man's wisdom. He taught that we should love our enemies and do good to those who hate us. He taught that we become great by being servants and that we find our lives by losing them. In the resurrection, we now see just how true those things are. He said that hearing his words and putting them into practice is like building our houses on rock, but going any other way is like building on sand. This message is now vindicated. The Greek mathematician Archimedes, as he worked with a fulcrum, made the famous statement, "Give me a place to stand, and I will move the earth." The resurrection gives us a place to stand. We now know what is true.

Second, the resurrection shows that the kingdom of God has in fact come. If Jesus could say during his ministry, "But if I drive out demons by the finger of God, then the kingdom of God has come to you" (Luke 11:20), what does it mean now that something much more mighty has happened? What does it mean now that much more than pesky demons have been cast out, but that the last enemy has been destroyed? Hasn't the kingdom now come with even greater force? Indeed, in his death and the resurrection, the kingdom had come with power. The future had broken into the present. There would still be a "not yet" quality regarding the kingdom, as the kingdom in its final form would have to wait for the age to come. However, in the resurrection of Jesus, the kingdom of God has been demonstrated on earth in the most powerful way possible in this age. The kingdom has come and a relationship with the extravagantly generous God, whom Jesus described, is offered to all men and women. Can God really be this good and as concerned about our lives as Jesus said? The resurrection proves he is.

Third, the resurrection demonstrates that God fully intends to continue what was started in the ministry of Jesus. Jesus' personal work on earth was completed, but it merely laid the foundation for what the resurrected Jesus would do through his church—until this good news of the kingdom reached the ends of the earth. Because of the resurrection, the story does not end in Palestine, but the message is spread to the nations. Twenty centuries later, the ministry of Jesus continues, still propelled by the resurrection. At some point in your life, someone probably befriended you and shared some of this story with you. Perhaps you have already embraced it and are now telling it to others. This is all because of the resurrection.

Because of the resurrection, you and I can be sure that God is still at work in our world. I can remember in the 1960s hearing much about "The Death of God Movement"—not exactly a movement that would inspire its followers. Started by a seminary professor at Emory University, it made the cover of *Time* magazine. But "The Death of God Movement" is, yes, now dead. God's work in the world, however, goes on.

The resurrection is his clear statement that what was begun in Jesus will be carried on. In one of his letters, Paul described how the power of resurrection continues with believers:

> I pray also that the eyes of your heart may be enlightened in order that you may know the hope to which he has called you, the riches of his glorious inheritance in the saints, and his incomparably great power for us who believe. That power is like the working of his mighty strength, which he exerted in Christ when he raised him from the dead and seated him at his right hand in the heavenly realms. (Ephesians 1:18–20)

Fourth, the resurrection means that those who follow him will also share in his resurrection. We have noted the "now/not yet" quality of the kingdom of God. In a similar way, there is a "now/not yet" quality for the resurrection in the lives of disciples. Those who follow Jesus deny themselves, lose their lives and become the seeds that fall into the ground and die. Paul will later speak of how disciples are those who have "died with Christ" (Romans 6:8), but he will quickly go on to say that those who have died with him, will live with him (Romans 6:4, 5, 8). Those who follow Jesus share *now* in his resurrection. In this world they are the ones who "have tasted the goodness of the word of God and the powers of the coming age" (Hebrews 6:5). They are enjoying now a resurrected life. This new life, however, is being lived out in a fallen and imperfect world. Those who have been raised with Christ still sin and still feel the effects of others' sin. They still hurt and struggle, groan and die. But they live in hope, looking forward to the final resurrection when all that is mortal will be completely swallowed up by life. (See Paul's discussion of this in 2 Corinthians 4:16–5:5.) Though they are sharing in the resurrected life now, a day is coming when the dead in Christ will be finally raised and that which is perishable will put on the imperishable. (See Paul's message in 1 Corinthians 15:51–54.) The resurrection of Jesus is the guarantee that this will become reality for all those who follow him.

No examination of Jesus' life could possibly be complete without a serious look at the resurrection. Without the resurrection, Jesus and his message would have been buried somewhere in ancient history. If there had been no resurrection, there would have been no New Testament written about him, and there would have been no church that would have spread his word. If there had been no resurrection, we would not find Jesus on the cover of *Time* magazine in the twenty-first century. "He is risen!" his disciples proclaimed. The evidence is abundant. The implications are monumental—for each of us.

# Disciples of Jesus

From time to time, after reading unusual articles in magazines or seeing documentaries on television, I have just a three word response: "That is amazing!" People do things with their lives that are quite astonishing. There are heroic stories and accounts of creativity and perseverance that are remarkable. But seldom do those stories require anything of me; I can feel amazed and then go on my way to the next event in my life. A story may be fascinating enough that I will recount it to some friends at dinner, but normally, I don't make any major changes in my life because of such things. Jesus' story is amazing and his message is remarkable, but he did not come just to amaze. He came to call men and women to embrace his message, to make major changes and to follow him in adopting a whole new approach to life.

His first followers were described as disciples. The word meant a learner or a pupil and was used in many contexts to describe those who adhered to the message of a teacher or leader. Jesus talked throughout his ministry about those who would become his disciples, what was involved in being his disciple, and how some people were going to make choices that would mean they could not be his disciples. As he spoke, it became quite clear that he had something very specific in mind when he used the word "disciple." In our examination of his life and his teachings, we have already seen elements of

that message, but in this chapter we will look more specifically at the idea of being his disciple.

## The Most Serious Commitment

When we examine carefully those texts in which Jesus calls
people to be disciples, we see quickly that what he has in mind
is a drastic thing. Since the kingdom of God is so
different, so good and so important, it is not really surprising
that being a part of it would represent a radical and far-reach-
ing decision, and this is exactly the way Jesus presents it.

Jesus can never be accused of surprising people with the
fine print of the contract. He let his hearers know, in the most
up-front way, that life with him would be all-consuming.
There must be a complete end to token religion. "If any one
would come after me," he said, "let him deny himself and take
up his cross daily and follow me" (Luke 9:23). Followers of
Jesus were not asked to give a certain percentage—they were
ask to give up themselves. As Dietrich Bonhoeffer wrote,
"When Christ calls a man, he bids him come and die."[1] Jesus
was clear about two things: (1) the kingdom is the greatest
thing there is and (2) it will cost you everything you have to
be part of it. Every effort to work in Christian activities around
the edges of things we are more concerned about is an affront
to the gospel of the kingdom. "And anyone who does not carry
his cross and follow me," Jesus said, "cannot be my disciple"
(Luke 14:27). We can be sure that any attempt to soften this
message or to explain it away will result in something bearing
little resemblance to the kingdom as Jesus taught it.

One point here is hard to miss: We cannot be Jesus' disciples unless our commitment to him becomes the most serious
commitment in our lives. Jesus further illustrated this point

when he said that allegiance to him must surpass even commitment to family:

> "Anyone who loves his father or mother more than me is not worthy of me; anyone who loves his son or daughter more than me is not worthy of me; and anyone who does not take his cross and follow me is not worthy of me." (Matthew 10:37–38)

Jesus purposely chose words that would quickly communicate the seriousness of his message to his first-century audience. Loyalty to family was a sacred obligation. However, if men and women are going to be disciples, they must love him more. We make a serious mistake, however, if we think Jesus is asking disciples not to love their families. What I hear is a call for disciples to put their love for family in a larger context, in the context of an all-surpassing love they have for God and for his kingdom. As a son, a husband and a father, I understand something of the devotion, concentration and perseverance that these roles require. Jesus calls me to have all of these qualities, but first to have them in my relationship to him. By doing this, I will find the power and direction to be faithful to my other relationships.

## Affecting Everything

Jesus finished his call to discipleship in Luke 14 with these words: "In the same way, any of you who does not give up everything he has cannot be my disciple" (Luke 14:33). I suppose that we could read this to literally mean that a person or a family must sell everything or give it all away. However, there are several reasons to think he means something different. First, such action would accomplish nothing, except putting a person or his family on the welfare roll.

Second, this is not a practice that we ever see taking place in the early church. Third, there could hardly be a functioning group that would be able to make an impact on the world if everyone in it completely divested himself of all belongings and wealth. Fourth, this would assume Jesus was only concerned about our possessions when in fact his interests are much broader. It is much better, but no less radical, to understand instead that everything is to be put under the lordship of Jesus. Nothing is to be left out or excluded; every area of a disciple's life is to be brought under Jesus' control.

In my experience, I have found that many people want to be religious and want a connection with God, but they do not want this connection to affect certain areas of their lives. They want the freedom to handle certain things the way they choose, while still involving themselves spiritually in matters that appeal to them. This is precisely what Jesus is saying we cannot do and still be disciples.

Think about some of the things "everything" would involve: money, houses, cars, businesses, education, family, relationships, attitudes, ambitions, desires, time, personality traits. Jesus is saying that *everything* must be given up to him. He then has the freedom to discard what he doesn't want and control and direct everything else. Those who chafe at this idea either are not in touch with what pride and selfishness do to us or lack the confidence that whoever loses his life for Jesus' sake really does find it. Only those who are ready to let Jesus affect everything can be his disciples.

## For All People

Many years ago I had a discussion with a man forty years my senior who had been a leader in a church for quite some time. After hearing me speak on Jesus' message of discipleship in Luke 14, he suggested to me that I change my approach. "There are many younger Christians and many non-Christians," he said, "who are just not ready for this message that calls for a total commitment." I suspect there are others who feel the way he did. But when we look at whom Jesus was speaking to in Luke 14:25–35, we find that it was to "large crowds." These strong words calling for a radical commitment were not spoken to a few select individuals that Jesus thought were ready for the "tough talk" about discipleship. Surely there were all kinds of people in those crowds: spiritual veterans and spiritual newcomers, rich and poor, healthy and ill, married and single, young and old. For all these people there was the one message about discipleship: Jesus expected them to be totally committed to him and to the kingdom.

The old had to take up the cross as well as the young. The poor had to take up the cross as well as the rich. The unhealthy man would not be exempt from the cross just because he was not as well as someone else. In his own way, he too would have to take the cross or else he could not be a disciple. This does not mean, of course, that God fails to take into account our differences in ability and strength and energy. Certainly, different people in different life situations will have different opportunities, but Jesus calls everyone to have the same attitude and the same heart.

## A Supreme Concern

We have seen that Jesus described himself as one who came to seek and to save those who were lost (Luke 19:10), but at the close of Matthew's Gospel, we see what he wanted all lost people to become:

> Then Jesus came to them and said, "All authority in heav-
> en and on earth has been given to me. Therefore go and
> make disciples of all nations, baptizing them in the name of
> the Father and of the Son and of the Holy Spirit, and teach-
> ing them to obey everything I have commanded you. And
> surely I am with you always, to the very end of the age."
> (Matthew 28:18–20)

As the resurrected Jesus sent out his followers to proclaim his
message, their mission was clear: to make disciples. Jesus'
goal was not to get people out of one religion into another or
to swell the ranks of religious worshipers. He was supremely
concerned that all men and women become his disciples with
the understanding of that term, which he had been teaching
throughout his ministry. For Jesus, the only appropriate and
valid response to the good news of the kingdom was to
repent, turn away from an old way of living, and embrace the
life and lifestyle of a disciple. This means becoming one who
is constantly learning to more closely follow Jesus' teaching.

It is not uncommon in many religious circles to find the
idea that there are two types of Christians: first, the normal,
garden variety and second, those with extraordinary commitment who are "disciples." When we find this kind of thinking,
we of course find the widely held idea that we can be
Christians without being disciples. In other words, we can be
Christians in decent standing without being so seriously committed to the message of Jesus. There is not a hint of this idea
in any of Jesus' teachings, and there is plenty of evidence that
he would have found it to be abhorrent. To those in his day
who may have entertained some similar thoughts, he said:
"Why do you call me, 'Lord, Lord,' and do not do what I say?"
(Luke 6:46). Others were warned with these words:

"Many will say to me on that day, 'Lord, Lord, did we not prophesy in your name, and in your name drive out demons and perform many miracles?' Then I will tell them plainly, 'I never knew you. Away from me, you evildoers!'" (Matthew 7:22–23)

Jesus brought a message of unparalleled good news, but he knew that the only ones who could possibly benefit from it were those who responded as disciples. It would be foolish to think that he was just being arbitrarily hard at this point. The nature of the kingdom of God is such that you cannot find it or enjoy it until you treat it as the treasure in the field that is worth everything you have.

Jesus' words here in Matthew 28 make something else absolutely clear. Those who become his disciples and are devoted to obeying all that he commanded, will, in their own generation, embrace the command to make disciples. They can never be content just to have found the kingdom themselves. They must help others find it. They must bring others to an understanding of what it means to put all of life under Jesus' control. It is impossible to take seriously the message of Jesus and not accept the mission of helping others to become disciples.

The task of making a disciple does not end when someone is baptized and enters the kingdom. If you will forebear one technicality, in the Greek text here in Matthew 28:19–20, "baptizing them...and teaching them to obey everything I have commanded you" are participial phrases modifying the main verb, "make disciples." Obviously, there will be certain teaching leading to baptism, but the making of a disciple is an ongoing process in which the person continues to be taught all the ways Jesus' message affects our lives. Once we have decided to follow Jesus, his supreme concern must become our concern; we too must see the need to make disciples.

## Counting the Cost

When we come face to face with the reality of Jesus and his message, the question should not be, "Is this hard or is it easy?" The question should be, "Is it true?" If it is true, all debate should theoretically stop. But life is not lived in the realm of the theoretical. The truth is, Jesus' message is hard for us, and because of this, we struggle with it. But this struggle is not bad; he described it as "counting the cost" (Luke 14:28, 31).

Jesus' message is so different from our natural inclinations. It requires faith. It calls for big changes. It is a narrow road. It makes us uncomfortable. And yet, his message is in response to the kingdom and the extravagant generosity of God. It costs us everything, but it gives us a hundredfold in return. We lose our lives, but we find them. As a young adult seeking Jesus, I found Dietrich Bonhoeffer's words about "costly grace" to be most inspiring and helpful:

> Such grace is *costly* because it calls us to follow, and it is *grace* because it calls us to follow *Jesus Christ*. It is costly because it costs a man his life, and it is grace because it gives a man the only true life. It is costly because it condemns sin, and grace because it justifies the sinner.[2]

Hardly anything in this chapter says what we would have hoped Jesus would say. Taking up a cross. Giving him loyalty above family. Yielding everything. These are big challenges.

But a serious problem calls for radical surgery. To find a new life, you have to die to an old one. I referred earlier to the tension between the "unbelievables" and the "undeniables." We may think it is almost unbelievable that Jesus would make such radical demands of us. But once his reality is undeniable, then we have a big reason to take a huge step in response.

# But Does It Work?

Thus far, we have focused primarily on the material we find in the Gospels about who Jesus was, what he taught and what he did. The message we have examined is quite amazing. Jesus tells of a God who is good and is on our side. He tells of a God known for his expansive generosity. He calls for us to give up everything for his sake, but he promises that he can bring us into a relationship with a God who gives much more.

I thought seriously about ending this book with the previous chapter. But then I began to think about people going through all kinds of challenging circumstances, and I wondered, "But what will they think of this Jesus?" My greatest concern is that some people may say, "This sounds good and it seems reasonable that Jesus is all he claimed to be, but I am not really sure the message can work in my life." I said at the outset that this is not just a book about a great man, but a book about what that man teaches us about life. If you were to finish this book thinking this message cannot really connect with your life and your needs, then I will have fallen short of my goal.

## Life Is Difficult

Knowing the way many of us think, I can see some people coming to this point and wondering if Jesus was a bit out of touch. Was he so enthusiastic about the love of God that he forgot just how difficult and challenging life can be? Was he unrealistic to think that people going through great trials could still find joy in the kingdom of God? Did he perhaps not live long enough to see all that life can throw at us?

In the last two years I have seen the deaths of four men who were all special to me, none of whom was more than fifty-five years old. They all left behind wives who loved them. These couples had looked forward to more years together, to watching their children marry and to being grandparents together. What does Jesus' message say to these women and their families?

Because I have multiple sclerosis, a progressive chronic illness, I am frequently in touch with people facing a bewildering number of physical challenges. One person I know has diabetes, blindness due to the diabetes, cancer and kidney failure. I once heard her describe her almost unbelievable list of doctor's appointments for six months. The week I wrote this chapter, she had a kidney transplant.

My wife and I had lunch during the week of this writing with a couple from another state. It appears that mercury poisoning may be responsible for the fact that, although the wife is only in her thirties, she has had cataract surgery and has experienced major hearing loss and other symptoms of aging. As a mom of two small children, she is finding each day to be difficult.

The day before this chapter was written, I was on the phone with a man in his forties in the Midwest who has been disabled for ten years. Diagnosed with multiple sclerosis years ago, his doctors have just concluded that he actually has another illness which may be even more difficult to treat.

The list of challenging situations is almost endless. I see single moms struggling to meet the complex needs of raising their children. I see people who are overwhelmed with their financial situations. I see marriages distressed by deep-rooted and long-standing problems. I see stubborn psychological disorders. And of course, I am only looking at the world through my very limited First World glasses. There are problems in other countries that seem to have even more magnitude. By bringing all these things up, I am taking a risk that I may remind you of life's difficulties, causing you to forget the man and the message we have just considered. But I would not be giving you much credit if I did not acknowledge that you see all these things as well as I do and probably experience some of them first hand.

Is the message of Jesus just material for a fascinating theological study, or is there something here that can speak to me, my friends and countless others like us, as we come to grips with developments in life that are far different than what we would have hoped?

Let me frankly acknowledge that these are tough issues—and tough issues do affect the way we think. As each of these widows I mentioned works through her grief, she will probably not read Jesus' parable of the hidden treasure the same way she read it ten years ago. The response of women in midlife with children still to raise may be more muted. I know that my struggle with a disease that has a way of greatly complicating life, causes me to see many things through different eyes. As I write this, a CD in my computer is playing songs I have not listened to in years. They are from a favorite spiritual group from the 1970s. A friend with an old-fashioned turntable and some modern digital equipment recently burned the disc for me, and it has brought back many memories. A song titled "He Is the Way, the Truth and the Life" just ended. I cannot help thinking that when I listened to that song thirty years ago, life was much simpler. I have certainly seen a lot of challenges as the years have passed. Is the Gospel still as powerful?

## But Jesus

With these thoughts in mind, let us look again at Jesus. First, he was not out of touch with the difficulties of life. I think he knew exactly how hard life can be. He connected emotionally with the crowds who were "harassed and helpless, like sheep without a shepherd" (Matthew 9:36). He felt the pain of the lepers, the blind and the lame. For much of his ministry, he was very focused on the horrific way his own life would end. He had no illusions about the seriousness of life's challenges.

Second, Jesus had a clear vision of the love and generosity of God. He knew that in the end, this would carry the day—no matter how great the difficulties we might face. The good news of the kingdom is that the love of God cannot be stopped. "In this world," he said, "you will have trouble. But take heart! I have overcome the world" (John 16:33). Jesus did not declare an end to evil, pain or suffering during this life. He did, however, declare that for those who accept God's invitation, these things will not ultimately endure and they will not win.

Third, by declaring that the kingdom was breaking into the present age, Jesus was letting us know that resources are now present to help us and sustain us until the kingdom comes in all its fullness. When we are going through difficult times, nothing means more to us than relationships, and

Jesus assures us first that we would have a relationship with God where we would be respected, heard and loved. He did not promise no dark days or nights, but that there would be no darkness that could take us out of reach our *Abba,* Father. Beyond this relationship, he was forming a fellowship where his disciples would love one another as he had loved. Few people, if any, will escape difficulties. But what a difference it makes to have people around us who care. Death, illness, stress and disappointment will come to us all, but in Jesus we find a company of believers who are taught to love one another through those times and to encourage each other's faith.

## The Power of a New Perspective

Later in the New Testament, the author of Hebrews twice calls on his readers to fix their thoughts and their eyes on Jesus (Hebrews 3:1, 12:2). Focusing on Jesus will not change any of the circumstances that we described earlier, at least not immediately. However, fixing our thoughts on Jesus and his message does give us a calm and steady point in the middle of various storms. The same writer speaks of Jesus' message being an "anchor for the soul" (Hebrews 6:19). Getting a different perspective makes an amazing difference in life. And this is just what setting our thoughts on Jesus does. It focuses us on higher truth. It connects us with eternal realities and reminds us that our present troubles are light and momentary. Such a focus also brings us back to what we most need to deal with: our own hearts. It reminds us of those things that we can change and those that we cannot. Is such a perspective easy to maintain? "Easy" would not be the word

I would choose. However, when we are convinced of the truth of Jesus' message, we have reason to fight to maintain it.

Yes, life is difficult, and Jesus' message would not be worth much if it did not deal with this. Nothing about his message would imply that these difficulties are illusory. Instead, his message and his story show that as real and painful as life can be, God will first sustain us through the pain and then he will bring good out of it. In the end, he will absolutely triumph over it.

*Epilogue*

# What Will *You* Do?

"What shall I do, then, with Jesus who is called Christ?" Pilate asked.

Matthew 27:22

hat will you do with this Jesus? If he does not already have you, there is every indication that he still has some plan to offer you God's extravagant generosity. It is evident that he is not going to go away. Two thousand years later, he is still showing up. How many attempts to reach you has he made in your life? You can avoid him for a while, but sooner or later he shows up again. There he is now, working afresh in an old friend you never thought was interested much in religion. There he is at a funeral for a coworker, his words tugging at your heart. There he is in a stranger who befriends you and then invites you to look into his teachings. Francis Thompson used the picturesque phrase "The Hound of Heaven" to describe him in his famous poem. He has your scent, and he keeps coming after you, not to cajole you or entrap you, but to give you yet another chance to sit at his banquet table, yet another chance to taste that he is, in fact, very good. What will you do with him?

There were those in the Gospels who had their chance, turned it down and went away, never to be heard from again. A bright young man had his chance. He was quite interested in Jesus, but more interested in his money. He went away sad.

We can assume that his situation eventually got worse. That is not what Jesus wanted—not for him, not for me, not for you. He came to offer you God's abundance. It will cost you everything. It will give you much more. The fact that you are reading this book and have actually made it all the way to the end probably means you are not far from the kingdom. Do I sense a party coming on?

## Who Are You?

Some who are reading this are new disciples. I have actually written an entire book just for you.[1] You are precious to God and precious to your brothers and sisters. You did the right thing. You understood the need to change, and you accepted God's gracious offer. You had the guts to stand before others and to declare "Jesus is Lord." Those words of yours echoed all the way to the corners of glory *and* into the dungeons of demons, because you stood face to face with the truth about God, the truth about yourself and the truth about this world; and you had the heart and the humility to admit how much you needed him. You put your faith in the right person. You committed to the right cause. And you will not be sorry. Already God is using you in the lives of many—even in the lives of those who seem much farther down the spiritual road than you. An amazing journey has just begun. Stay humble, stay honest and stay hungry. Spend the rest of your life learning more and more about this man, Jesus.

Some of you can remember when you were a new disciple. You can still remember what you felt as you came out of the waters of baptism. You once accepted Jesus' offer, but then something interfered. He spoke of thorns that would grow up and choke out the faith of those who had made a good beginning. He mentioned specifically the worries of life and the deceitfulness of wealth. These, for sure, can be major culprits, but he was not giving a complete list. Some have allowed painful relationships and mistakes by others to harden or embitter them.

Perhaps you still duck into a church occasionally or open your Bible on tough days, but because of some temporary, worldly matter or because of some human being or group of human beings, you no longer passionately seek the kingdom of God. You no longer joyfully submit to the Lord of life. Do you see the tragedy in this? Do you realize that the God Jesus described stands on the porch, waiting to run to you and put a ring and robe of honor on you and throw a party for you? Such "insane love" is more than a little embarrassing, especially when we all know that we deserve quite the opposite. But the Jesus who once announced the good news of the kingdom to us, is back to show us just how wide and long and high and deep the love of God is. He is so ready to forgive and so ready to have you again at the banquet table. It will take humility to come back, but that has always been at the heart of following Jesus.

And what about those who made a decision to accept Jesus and his kingdom and have never left? You are not going anywhere. You believe Jesus has the answers. Like the disciples, you say to Jesus, "To whom shall we go? You have the words of eternal life" (John 6:68). But something is missing. You no longer look like you are connected to resurrection power. Somewhere in the daily grind of life, you have lost touch with the abundance of God. More importantly, maybe you have lost faith that you can ever experience it again. It is not, however, a tired and disappointed Jesus who comes to you, weary with your sluggish heart. It is not a Jesus who just has enough to give one more weak word of encouragement. It is the One who gladly died for us and still has one goal for us: to infuse us with his life. The letter to the Hebrews gives us a good indication of the kinds of encouragement he might give to us. (Obviously, these texts have been slightly changed to put the words on Jesus lips and in some cases to emphasize the meaning.)

> "You have come to share in me if you hold firmly till the end the confidence you had at first." (See Hebrews 3:14.)

> "In me you do not have a high priest who is unable to sympathize with your weaknesses, but you have one who has been tempted in every way, just as you are—yet was without sin. Now you can approach the throne of [boundless] grace with confidence, and receive mercy and find [extravagant] grace to help you in your time of need." (See Hebrews 4:15-16.)

> "I am not unjust; I have not forgotten your work and the love you have shown me as you have helped my people and continue to help them. I want each of you to show this same diligence to the very end, in order to make your hope sure." (See Hebrews 6:10-11.)

> "See to it that you don't miss the [lavish] grace of God. [I am just as eager to give it to you today as at the beginning.]" (See Hebrews 12:15.)

While God stands waiting, with arms full of grace and the resources needed to revitalize our hearts and minds, renewing our relationship with him always comes through *metanoia*—repentance. Whenever the connection with God's abundance is lost, someone will always need to repent, and the someone will not be God. But when we humbly take ownership of our sin and let that lead us to repentance, it will always bring "times of refreshing from the Lord." When Peter proclaimed this to a Jerusalem crowd, he knew from personal experience just how true it was (Acts 3:20). He had learned the hard way just how deep God's wells of mercy really are and how complete his restorative power. If you have been Jesus' disciple for a long time, he is eager to show you once again how fresh and full your walk with him can be!

I suppose this only leaves one group of people: those who are still celebrating the amazing fact that we have been loved by God, served by Christ, filled with the Holy Spirit, and added to the family of believers. Every day has not been a party. You have gone through some difficult times—some of your own making, some because of the failures of others, and some just because of the way life works out. But by the grace of God, you are still rejoicing that your name is written in heaven. You are too aware of your sinful nature to think that you can take credit for where you are; you know you have been justified by grace through faith. You understand that you have not finished the race. You know that there is an enemy who would love to knock you out, especially after a long and fruitful run. But with another disciple of Jesus, you say:

> I want to know Christ and the power of his resurrection and the fellowship of sharing in his sufferings, becoming like him in his death, and so, somehow, to attain to the resurrection from the dead.
>
> Not that I have already obtained all this, or have already been made perfect, but I press on to take hold of that for which Christ Jesus took hold of me. Brothers, I do not consider myself yet to have taken hold of it. But one thing I do: Forgetting what is behind and straining toward what is

ahead, I press on toward the goal to win the prize for which
God has called me heavenward in Christ Jesus. (Philippians
3:10-14)

I decided thirty-five years ago to follow this Jesus. What I
really decided, although I didn't understand it at the time, was
to let Jesus open a storehouse of grace for me. He has fulfilled
his promises. He has blessed me with family. He has given me
friends. He has helped me grow up. He has forgiven me much
more than "seventy times seven" (Matthew 18:22). He has
guided me, and sometimes carried me, through some serious
storms. He has taught me how to have joy in trials. But more
than anything, he has shown me that his willingness to give
me grace is as unending as my need for it. Some tough
challenges surely lie ahead, but as a follower of his in a Nazi
concentration camp once observed, "No pit is so deep that he
is not deeper still."

I have decided to follow Jesus. And you?

# Notes

### Introduction: Jesus—The Hinge of Your History

1. Thomas Cahill, *Desire of the Everlasting Hills: The World Before and After Jesus* (New York: Nan A. Talese, 1999).

### Chapter 1: Who Did He Think He Was?

1. "Who Was Jesus?" *Time*, August 12, 1988.

2. Quoted in Bruce Metzger, *The New Testament, Its Background, Growth and Content* (New York: Abingdon, 1965), 78.

3. Metzger, 78.

4. In another reference, Josephus actually identifies Jesus as the Messiah. But in view of one clearly negative description, it appears that this one may have been an interpolation of later Christian writers. See *Antiquities* 18.3.3 in *The Works of Josephus* (Peabody, Mass.: Hendrickson Publishers, Inc., 1987).

5. I have not written here about every claim that Jesus made. In addition to these that we have examined, we have his shocking statements about coming on the clouds with power and glory at the last day (Matthew 24:30, 26:64; Mark 13:26, 14:62). There is also his statement that he could call on his Father, who would put twelve legions of angels at his disposal, if he chose to be delivered from his impending trial and death (Matthew 26:53). The Gospel of John has the well-known "I Am" statements. In the most notable passage, Jesus says, "I tell you the truth, before Abraham was born, I am!" (John 8:58), thus identifying himself with God (the great I Am of the Old Testament). In other passages he says, "I am the bread of life" (6:35), "I am the gate for the sheep" (10:7), and "I am the good shepherd" who "lays down his life for the sheep" (John 10:11).

### Chapter 2: His Dependence on God

1. I found this idea in James Woodroof, *Between the Rock and a Hard Place* (Searcy, Arkansas: Bible House, 1989), 45–46.

2. Charles Edward Jefferson, *Jesus—the Same* (Billerica, Mass.: Discipleship Publications International, 1997), 87.

3. James G. S. S. Thomson, *The Praying Christ* (Grand Rapids: Eerdmans, 1959), 36.

4. Robert E. Coleman, *The Mind of the Master* (Old Tappan, N.J.: F. H. Revell Co., 1977), 37–45.

5. Coleman, 39.

6. Joachim Jeremias, *The Lord's Prayer* (Philadelphia: Fortress Press, 1964), 16.

7. Andrew Greeley, *The Jesus Myth* (Garden City, New York: Image Books, 1971), 86. When Greely uses the word "myth," he is quick to point out that he does not mean legend, but rather, a story that points to the deeper meaning of life.

8. Jeremias, 21.

9. Jeremias, 21.

## Chapter 3: His Servant Heart

1. Thomas Olbricht, *The Power to Be* (Austin, Texas: Sweet Publications, 1979).

2. C. H. Dodd, *The Founder of Christianity* (New York: Macmillan, 1970), 105.

3. Joachim Jeremias carefully analyzed five passages in the Gospels where Jesus applied the Servant songs to himself and concluded that the Servant theme was at the core of Jesus' message. Joachim Jeremias, *The Central Message of the New Testament* (New York: Charles Scribner's Sons, 1965), 45–46.

4. Coleman, 99.

## Chapter 4: Rich in Character

1. For a thorough study of the various aspects of his character, see Charles Edward Jefferson, *Jesus—the Same* (Billerica, Mass.: Discipleship Publications International, 1997). This fascinating

series of sermons was originally published in 1908 as *The Character of Jesus* but has been revised and reissued.

## Chapter 5: Jesus and the Scriptures

1. Coleman, 54.

2. Some might reason that since Jesus was the Incarnate Word, he had no need to learn the Scriptures. However, while there are certainly examples of Jesus having supernatural insight (for example, knowing what people were thinking), the New Testament does not seem to indicate that he gained his wisdom and knowledge supernaturally. Rather, he grew as others did (Luke 2:52) and learned as we all do (Hebrews 5:8).

## Chapter 6: The Kingdom of God

1. This material, not actually written by Solomon, is quoted in Dodd, 143.

2. Matthew actually uses the phrase "the kingdom of heaven" out of deference to his Jewish audience who would have preferred this when used in written form. All the other Gospel writers are united in using the phrase "the kingdom of God" which surely was what Jesus proclaimed.

3. Dodd, 115.

4. John Bright, *The Kingdom of God* (Nashville: Abingdon, 1952), 197.

5. Dodd, 147.

6. If you think you have the idea of kingdom all figured out, just take a look at the nine times in Matthew where Jesus says, "The kingdom is like…." I suspect that the variety of metaphors and parables will humble you, as they do me.

7. Bright, 217–218.

8. Whenever I consider the variety of images Jesus used for the kingdom, I find just another element of his teaching that makes me think of Philip Shaff's statement that "it would have taken more than Jesus to have invented Jesus." Philip Shaff, *History of the Christian*

*Church* (Grand Rapids: Eerdmans, 1962), 109. It stretches credulity to think that an uneducated crowd from Galilee could have manufactured the rich and paradoxical words of Jesus as some claim.

9. Cahill, 69.

10. Of the fifty-eight times this word occurs in either its verb or noun form in the New Testament, only five of those refer to repentance from some specific sin, and four of them are in Revelation. Only in Acts 8:22 where Simon the Sorcerer is told to "repent of this wickedness" do we find such use of the word outside of Revelation. In every other case—in the Gospels, Acts and the letters—the word would seem to refer to a more general change of heart and mind.

11. If any of this gets too technical, just skip to the last paragraph of this chapter. You can always come back to this later.

12. It has been suggested to me by other teachers whom I highly esteem that an alternative explanation of Mark 9:1 is that Jesus is here referring to the destruction of Jerusalem in 70 AD. This would mean that the kingdom "coming with power" (or the "Son of Man coming in his kingdom," as Matthew 16:28 puts it) would be God removing the old system of Judaism, leaving only his true kingdom on earth. Those offering this idea believe that comparing Matthew 16:28, Luke 21:5-32, Hebrews 12:25-29 and Hebrews 8:13 with the context of Mark 9:1 make this interpretation reasonable. However, they have been quick to say that either way, the point is the same: the kingdom comes in various ways at various times as God enters into history to change it for his people and his purposes. The establishment of the church in Acts 2 was certainly the high water mark, but not the only time or manner that God "came" in his kingdom.

13. I have found George Eldon Ladd's very thorough discussion of the relationship between the kingdom and the church to be most helpful. He organizes this discussion under five points: (1) The church is not the kingdom; (2) the kingdom creates the church; (3) the church witnesses to the kingdom; (4) the church is the instrument of the kingdom; (5) the church is the custodian of the kingdom. George Eldon Ladd, *A Theology of the New Testament* (Grand Rapids: Eerdmans, 1974), 105–119.

## Chapter 7: His Good News—Extravagant Generosity

1. Greely, 47.

2. Dodd, 65.

3. Greely, 47.

4. Greely, 47.

## Chapter 8: Kingdom Attitudes

1. It is sometimes noted that Jesus did not speak of grace, but that it was Paul who developed that idea. While Jesus did not use the word, the way he begins this sermon, combined with all that we looked at in the previous chapter, makes it clear that he understood and taught that man is justified not by his own efforts but by God's grace and generosity.

2. David Martyn Lloyd-Jones, *Studies in the Sermon on the Mount* (Grand Rapids: Eerdmans, 2001).

3. It is clear that a Christian leader like Paul understood this when we see his statements later in life, showing how he still saw himself as a sinner saved by grace (see 1 Corinthians 15:9–10; Ephesians 3:7–8; 1 Timothy 1:15).

4. Philip Yancey, in his often helpful book, *The Jesus I Never Knew* (Grand Rapids: Zondervan, 1995), feels comfortable rearranging the Beatitudes, so that he deals last with the "those who mourn." Such an approach takes the passages out of context and leaves us with a variety of interpretations.

5. Space will not allow me to devote as much attention to the remaining beatitudes as we did for the first two. I have developed the first two in greater detail, because it seems to me that they are the keys to all the others. Hopefully, examining these two will encourage readers to do similiar studies for the rest.

6. William Barclay, *The Gospel of Matthew*, Vol. 1 (Philadelphia: Westminster Press, 1956), 91–92.

7. For more on this topic see an excellent essay by Fred Faller, "Religious or Righteous?" *The Leaders Resource Handbook* (Billerica, Mass.: Discipleship Publications International, 1998), 143–147.

8. For more study on this theme, see Matthew 13:44–46, 22:34–40 and Philippians 3:7–11.

9. For more study on this theme see Mark 10:45; Ephesians 4:32; Philippians 2:1–7; 1 John 3:16.

10. For more study on this theme see 1 Samuel 16:7; Psalm 51; Jeremiah 17:9; Matthew 15:15–20; 1 Timothy 1:5; and Hebrews 3:12–13.

11. For more study on this theme see Jeremiah 6:13–15 (we should not be those who say "peace, peace" when there is no peace); Ephesians 2:13–18 (there is no peace unless people come to peace with God); and Matthew 28:18–20 (a description of what real peacemakers will do).

12. For more study on this theme see John 15:18–20; 2 Timothy 3:10–12; 1 Peter 4:3–4. We will also look more at persecution in chapter 10.

## Chapter 9: The Kingdom Lifestyle

1. Philip Yancey, *The Jesus I Never Knew* (Grand Rapids: Zondervan, 1995), 130.

2. Dodd, 68.

3. To read the description of this by a converted Pharisee who intimately knew what he was talking about, see Philippians 3:7–9.

## Chapter 10: Conflict and Controversy

1. William Barclay, *The Mind of Jesus* (New York: Harper and Row, 1960), 150.

2. Yancey, 90.

3. Barclay, 158.

## Chapter 11: Even Death on a Cross

1. Dodd, 141.

2. For example, Psalm 22 and Isaiah 53.

3. John Howard Yoder has written about how the world would be changed if Jesus had made another decision. He is right in assuming that Jesus could have chosen other than he did. The Gospel writers make it clear that he could have chosen not to go to the cross. John Howard Yoder, *The Politics of Jesus* (Grand Rapids: Eerdmans, 1972), 55–56.

4. Cahill, 285.

5. Cahill, 288.

6. For a more detailed examination of these sayings, see Oswald Sanders, *The Incomparable Christ* (Chicago: Moody Press, 1952), 155–200.

7. Sanders, 157.

## Chapter 12: The Empty Tomb

1. Ladd, 317.

2. Dodd, 169–170.

## Chapter 13: Disciples of Jesus

1. Dietrich Bonhoeffer, *The Cost of Discipleship* (New York: Macmillan, 1949), 99.

2. Bonhoeffer, 47.

## Epilogue: What Will *You* Do?

1. Thomas A. Jones, *Letters to New Disciples* (Billerica, Mass.: Discipleship Publications International, 1997).

# WHO ARE WE?

Discipleship Publications International (DPI) began publishing in 1993. We are a nonprofit Christian publisher affiliated with the International Churches of Christ, committed to publishing and distributing materials that honor God, lift up Jesus Christ and show how his message practically applies to all areas of life. We have a deep conviction that no one changes life like Jesus and that the implementation of his teaching will revolutionize any life, any marriage, any family and any singles household.

Since our beginning, we have published more than 125 titles; plus, we have produced a number of important, spiritual audio products. More than 1.8 million volumes have been printed, and our works have been translated into more than a dozen languages—international is not just a part of our name! Our books are shipped regularly to every inhabited continent.

To see a more detailed description of our works, find us on the World Wide Web at www.dpibooks.org. You can order books by calling 1-888-DPI-BOOK twenty-four hours a day. From outside the US, call 978-670-8840 during Boston-area business hours.

We appreciate the hundreds of comments we have received from readers. We would love to hear from you. Here are other ways to get in touch:

**Mail:** DPI, 2 Sterling Road, Billerica, Mass., 01862-2595
**E-Mail:** dpibooks@icoc.org

# FIND US ON THE WORLD WIDE WEB

www.dpibooks.org

1-888-DPI-BOOK

Outside the US, call

978-670-8840